Bridgwater

History and Guide

Bridgwater

History and Guide

Robert Dunning

ALAN SUTTON

First published in the United Kingdom in 1992 by
Alan Sutton Publishing Ltd
Phoenix Mill · Far Thrupp · Stroud · Gloucestershire

First published in the United States of America in 1993 by
Alan Sutton Publishing Inc · 83 Washington Street · Dover NH 03820

British Library Cataloguing in Publication Data

    Dunning, R.W.
    Bridgwater: History and Guide
    I. Title
    942.381

    ISBN 0-7509-0192-6

Jacket Illustration: Bridgwater (*Viewfinder Colour Photo Library*)

To John F. (Jack) Lawrence, who so generously shared his
knowledge and inspired so many by his enthusiasm, that the
people of Bridgwater are in no doubt about the riches of their
inheritance.

Typeset in 10/13 Times.
Typesetting and origination by
Alan Sutton Publishing Limited.
Printed in Great Britain by
The Bath Press, Avon.

Contents

CHAPTER ONE

The Parrett Valley

FROM THE FIRST SETTLERS TO THE NORMAN CONQUEST

The River Parrett, rising in the hilly country on the northern edge of Dorset, gives its name to North and South Perrott and South Petherton as it drains the lush pastures of the golden Ham stone country. Swollen by the Yeo and the Isle, it forces its way through the Langport Gap to the central basin known as the Somerset Levels. In the days before the great ecclesiastical landlords began their drainage schemes, the Parrett, joined by the Tone from the west and the Cary from the east, was often a torrent whose course to the sea was governed only by the ridge of hills later called the Poldens on the east, and by two much smaller ridges to the west. The polished stone axe found at Hamp and the Bronze Age urn from Colley Lane are but two reminders that man has been exploiting the Parrett and its hinterland for perhaps five thousand

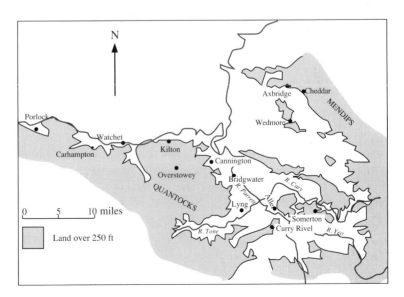

The Somerset Levels and the Parrett: the Saxon defences

years, crossing and recrossing the river long before the bridge was built and following tracks like the one along the ridge known as Wembdon Hill. On the high point of that hill traces of a triangular earthwork may be interpreted as a Bronze Age fortress commanding a route which crossed the river at Crowpill.

Another, smaller, ridge further south has a similar site near Durleigh, called Sturton's Castle in the sixteenth century after a former owner, and much later known as Danesborough. This may mark a second route from the Crowpill crossing.

But the Parrett must have been an uncomfortable neighbour, regularly breaching its banks and discouraging close association. As yet there is no evidence for any settlement by the river, even by the sophisticated Durotriges who occupied its valley in the years before the Roman occupation. The Romans, however, found the river a vital artery in their settlement and exploitation of the region. They established a significant port on the east bank at Crandon Bridge and a smaller one perhaps later on the west bank at Combwich. Crandon was evidently Bridgwater's predecessor as the entrepôt for much of the land to the east, probably the loading place for Mendip lead and the corn grown and stock raised on the villa estates as far away as Ilchester. Among local farms was one below Wembdon Hill at Perry Green. Roman coins found just inland from Crowpill show that travellers still used the ancient routes; and some small pieces of pottery dug up in King Square suggest that just possibly the site chosen for the great medieval castle of Bridgwater had been recognized as a safe place for settlement a thousand years earlier.

Both raiders and traders from the time of the Roman occupation, and probably much earlier, found that Somerset's western coast was accessible, and the West Saxon kings from Alfred onwards established both a formal chain of strongholds and a network of estates which could serve as military bases as well as political and economic centres of their power. Alfred owned Carhampton, Kilton and Cannington from which to defend his kingdom from coastal attack in the west, and the fortress at Lyng was later to form part of that system of national defence extended by his son and successor, Edward the Elder, which strengthened the western coast with the burh at Watchet and, together with other royal estates, encircled the vulnerable moors — Curry Rivel, the Somerton holding which stretched from Aller along the ridge to the Charltons, Cheddar, Axbridge, Wedmore and Burnham. Between coast and moor was the Parrett, potentially the weak point in the defences, its winding course by no means impassable to skilled navigators with vessels of shallow draught.

In 845, before Alfred's time, a Danish army was beaten off with great slaughter at the mouth of the river, by defenders drawn from Dorset as well as Somerset. In 914, despite a system of coastal defence stretching from Avonmouth to Cornwall, some survivors of an already defeated Viking army 'stole inland by night' east of Watchet and at Porlock. In 988 and 997 Watchet was again ravaged. In practice the coast was indefensible, a fact well appreciated by Harold, son of the exiled Earl Godwin, when he landed at Porlock in 1052 and defeated forces loyal to Edward the Confessor.

The land Harold recovered for his family almost certainly included a castle, now almost forgotten on the edge of Over Stowey village, which commanded a fine view of the coast at the Parrett mouth. The Confessor held Alfred's estate at Cannington, down in the valley, which controlled the ancient river crossing at Combwich, from which the *harepath* (military road) took its metalled course – hence 'stone way' and Stowey – to the Quantock ridge passing Harold's castle. The king also held the great minster parish of North Petherton, probably already associated with the royal forest of Quantock. And commanding a long stretch of the Parrett itself in 1066 were the estates of Bridgwater, Wembdon and Bawdrip, securely in the hands of Merlesuain, the sheriff of Lincolnshire, whom Harold was to leave in charge of the North in 1066.

THE MEDIEVAL LORDS AND THEIR ESTATES

Much the same strategic considerations occurred to the Conqueror. By 1086 two faithful followers, Alfred of Spain and Roger de Courcelles, held much of the land between the Parrett and the Quantocks; William de Mohun, the new sheriff of Somerset, was strong on the west coast. The eastern coast and both banks of the Parrett almost up to the boundary of North Petherton were entrusted to Walter or Walschin of Douai. Walter's huge block of land, reaching east across the moors almost to the Mendips, did not remain as a single unit for long. Within a generation or so most was held by others, but Bridgwater, Bower, Horsey, Wembdon and Pawlett were kept together, passing on Walter's death about 1107 to his son Robert of Bampton. After Robert's rebellion in 1136 they passed to his daughter Gillian and to her successive husbands Fulk Pagnell and Warin de Aule. Warin held them in 1166 and Fulk's son, also Fulk, before 1185. The younger Fulk went into exile in 1185 and did not recover his property until 1199, when he exchanged it with a Devon landowner, William Brewer.

These five holdings continued to be linked together until Brewer's son's death in 1233; and they were said to have a special relationship which probably went back to the days of Walter of Douai. Four of them were said to be held, in feudal language, as of the fifth, Bridgwater. And Bridgwater was administered directly by Walter himself. Was there already a stronghold on that ridge beside the river which provided a feudal focus at the heart of the Parrett valley?

The interpretation of the name Bridgwater has been a matter of debate. It used to be accepted that the name, spelt *Brugie* in Domesday, signified a bridge, and that the later form, *Brigewaltier*, in use by the end of the twelfth century, indicated that the bridge was built by Walter of Douai. There is, however, no other evidence for a bridge at that early date; and in the later Middle Ages it was William Brewer and not Walter who was thought to have been the builder of the Great Bridge, probably about 1200. Another, and more acceptable, view is that the name *Brugie* derives either from the Old English *brycg*, meaning a gang plank between ship and shore, or even from the Old Norse *bryggja*, meaning a quay or jetty.

'Walter's quay' does not, of course, imply a town. Domesday *Brugie* was an agricultural settlement surrounded by similar estates, whose names described their physical form. The flat grasslands each side of the Parrett are the 'hams' of the later Hamp and Sydenham; where the river seems often to have changed its course an island was formed, where horses grazed, hence Horsey; Pignes was probably the ridge of gravel around which the river flowed, and which therefore looked like a headland.

View of Bridgwater from the north. Note the glass kiln. Etching by J. Chubb, *c.* 1800

To the west of 'Walter's quay', towards the Quantocks, there was still much ancient woodland and the place-names suggest even more: Wembdon may be the 'hill of the huntsman', Durleigh the 'deer wood'; while Haygrove recalls the 100 acres of woodland recorded in Domesday *Brugie* which William Brewer was licensed to enclose in 1200 and out of which he or his son formed a deer park. And both east and west of Bridgwater were what seem to have been isolated farming hamlets, the Bowers, perhaps named after the small dwellings in which their inhabitants lived.

The medieval parish of Bridgwater touched Chedzoy and Bawdrip in the east and North Petherton in the south along natural boundaries that often followed streams. To the west and north there were complications where the parish interlocked with Durleigh, Wembdon and Chilton Trinity in such a way as to suggest that all were once part of a single estate, in which the sharing of grasslands, surviving as Chilton Common until the nineteenth century, defied all rational division. Until this century Bridgwater's history was confined within its ancient parish, but the town's expansion has now taken it into Wembdon ancient parish in Sydenham and Newtown; into Durleigh and Chilton along Chilton Road; into Durleigh again beyond Haygrove; and in the 1990s south across the boundary into Huntworth in North Petherton.

Within Bridgwater ancient parish by the time of Domesday (1086) there were four known estates. The most important was Walter of Douai's *Brugie*, which was worth £7. To the north-east was Horsey, which Rademar held of Walter, worth £4. Rademar also held Bower,

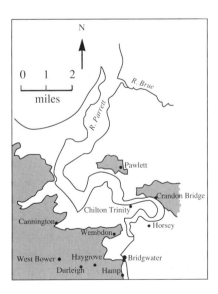

The division of land between the Parrett and the Quantocks

probably West Bower, worth 40*s*. In the south was Hamp, held since 1009 by Athelney Abbey and worth 30*s*.

Domesday Book records in its own inimitable way these four agricultural holdings. *Brugie*, the largest, paid geld for five hides (perhaps 600 arable acres), although there was land for ten plough-teams. The rest of the estate was worked by tenant farmers sharing eight plough-teams. There was land for seven teams at Horsey, where the home farm was very small and most of the land was worked with the tenants' five teams. Hamp was about half the size of Horsey and was shared almost equally between the lord and the tenant farmers. Bower, too, was shared equally. On the four estates together there were twenty-five tenants described as villeins, twenty-four as bordars, nine as cottars; and eleven *servi* belonged to the home farms. Those home farms between them supported forty-eight pigs, 111 sheep and forty 'beasts', and one riding horse was recorded at Horsey. Apart from the arable already noted, there were only 25 acres of pasture recorded for the whole parish, with none at all at Bower and Hamp.

Those four Domesday estates changed in different ways in the course of the next five centuries. Hamp belonged to Athelney Abbey until 1539, and its profits were paid to the abbey pittancer for distribution to the monks for their clothing and shoes. Rents from one farm paid for a lamp on the Lady chapel altar in the abbey church. In 1541 the Crown sold the manor to Bristol corporation. The overlordship of Horsey manor passed from William Brewer the younger in 1233 to his niece and eventually to the duchy of Lancaster. The effective owner by 1166 was William of Horsey, and his family remained in possession until the death of Sir Ralph Horsey in 1612. In the thirteenth and fourteenth centuries the home farm of about 130 acres was mostly arable. In 1327 there were at least twelve customary tenants, and ten years later nine of them paid extra rent instead of performing labour services. There was a windmill on the estate by 1294, the site of which was destroyed when the M5 motorway was built.

Bower is less easy to understand, because by the early thirteenth century Jordan of Chilton had land in 'his Bower', Little Bower and 'the other Bower'; and by 1318 Margery Godwin held land both in North and South Bower. West Bower can be traced with certainty back to 1280 and perhaps to one of the Bowers that Jordan held. None of these seem to have been large estates until the fifteenth century, when William Godwin the elder owned Godwinsbower. When another William died in 1502 his son Christopher succeeded to a manor house, which was apparently near St John's hospital in Eastover.

By the early sixteenth century there were two manors of North Bower, one owned by the Michel family of Gurney Street in Cannington, the other by the Perymans. West Bower came to the Cokers of Wembdon by 1335 and the surviving wing of the medieval manor house may have been built by Margaret Coker and her first husband, the lawyer Sir Alexander Hody (d. 1461). Margaret's heir was her cousin John Seymour, grandfather of both Jane Seymour, queen of Henry VIII, and of Edward Seymour, Duke of Somerset. On Edward's execution for treason in 1552 the manor passed to the Crown.

Apart from the main manor of Bridgwater, there were two other substantial estates in the Middle Ages. One had been created at Dunwear by the 1190s, when it was owned by Geoffrey the cook; by 1236 it had passed to the Raleigh family and from them by marriage in 1402 to the Chichesters of Beggearnhuish in Nettlecombe. The Chichesters owned Dunwear and one of the North Bower estates until 1660. The other was the property of St John's hospital, concentrated from 1215 in one block, called Hundred Acres. The hospital also owned the tithes of the parish and from 1349 some house properties in the town. When it was dissolved in 1539 its land was eventually acquired by the Colles family, and the tithes by Bridgwater corporation.

At the centre of the parish at the time of Domesday was Walter of Douai's estate, called *Brugie*. It passed on his death about 1107 to his son Robert of Bampton, and through Robert's daughter Gillian and her first husband Fulk Pagnell to their son, also Fulk Pagnell. Fulk the younger fled the realm in 1185 and the Crown held custody until 1199, when Fulk exchanged his Bridgwater estate with William Brewer. Brewer died in 1226, and his son and namesake in 1233. The huge Brewer estate was then divided between the elder William's three granddaughters. Bridgwater, which by this time included both a castle and a growing borough, was divided unequally between two of them, Maud and Eve de Braose.

Maud married into the powerful Mortimer family and her share was the castle and one-third of the borough and manor. This property passed through the Mortimer family, often held by widows, and on the death of Anne Mortimer in 1432 came to Richard Plantagenet, Duke of York, father of King Edward IV. Richard's widow Cecily remained lady of Bridgwater until her death in 1495. From that time a succession of royal ladies, including five of Henry VIII's wives, held the share as part of their jointures until the death of Catherine Parr in 1548.

Eve de Braose received as her share two-thirds of the borough and manor and took it to her husband William de Cauntelo. Their daughter Millicent married Eudes la Zouche, and successive barons Zouche were lords of that share of Bridgwater until 1485. Giles, Lord Daubeney, was then granted the estate by the Crown, and in 1508 was succeeded by his son Henry, who spent most of his fortune on acquiring the title of Earl of Bridgwater. The title cost him the estate, which he was forced to sell to Edward Seymour, owner of West Bower.

After the creation of the borough and the building of the castle about 1200, the land outside the growing town began to be regarded as a separate property, and by the end of the thirteenth century was often known as the manor of Haygrove. In 1249 the Mortimer family share comprised a home farm of 115 acres, rents from tenant farmers, and some cash payments instead of labour, the whole valued at £21 2s 10^1/$_2$$d$. The other share in 1256–7 had nearly 140 acres of oats, wheat, beans, rye and barley on the home farm. Two ploughmen and a carter were employed regularly and the rest of the labour was provided by nineteen tenant farmers, who also paid rent for their holdings. Sales of surplus grain, stock and pasture made a handsome profit; the gross income was £85 4s 11d.

Almost a century later the farming pattern on the Mortimer land had changed. The home farm land was nearly all let, and the rent income was £23 1s 7d. A small amount of that was from the sale of wax, paid as a tax called chevage. Accounts from the Zouche share have not survived and there are only rare later glimpses from Mortimer records. In 1381-2 and later, crops were lost because of flooding around Crowpill, and in the summer of 1413, estate income was slightly reduced because herons and sparrowhawks had not nested and because bees and rabbits had disappeared.

But if such details are rare, the general look of the land to the north and west of the town is clear. Apart from the park which William Brewer created and the Zouches maintained there were the common arable fields: Blackland in Crowpill in the north and, outside the town's west gate, North field, Matthew's field and Hayle or Hay field. These fields, still cultivated in the traditional way in the sixteenth century, were the survivors of a time before Bridgwater was ever a town.

CHAPTER TWO

The Town is Born, 1200–1400

THE CASTLE

Bridgwater's history as a town begins in the year 1200, when King John granted two charters to his faithful supporter William Brewer, one allowing him to build a castle, the other creating a borough outside its walls. A third charter, almost as important, licensed William to hold markets and fairs there. The effect of the first two charters was to allow Brewer to build a fortress, to control the strategic river crossing and to give shelter to what in little more than a century had changed from a rural village to a river port with great potential.

The castle never, perhaps, fulfilled its promise, although while he lived the Crown had no more loyal supporter than Brewer, who was at the heart of political affairs beside his king when Magna Carta was drawn up, who led the royal army against some of the barons, and loyally served the young Henry III until his death in 1226. But the castle played no direct part in these events although the restless King John presumably stayed there on visits to the town in 1204, 1205, 1208 and 1210. On the death of the second William Brewer in 1233 the vast estate was at first taken into Crown custody. The castle proved useful both as a prison and as a store; a safe place to hold cash taken as taxes until it should be needed. For that reason the royal constable was ordered in 1242 to repair the mound on which the keep stood, to mend turrets, and to make other necessary repairs. Four years later an order was given to renew the surrounding palisade and to roof the towers. Some of these orders seem to imply a timber fortress; what still survives is the early thirteenth-century water gate, providing direct access to and from the west quay, and a substantial length of strong stone curtain wall. Where the keep stood is as yet unknown. One other building inside the castle was the chapel of St Mark, complete by 1219 and where in 1535 a priest still celebrated Mass

The castle and West Quay, showing part of the curtain wall. The thirteenth-century Water Gate stands in the alley beside the Town House Hotel

three times a week for William Brewer the elder and King John.

The Mortimer family was as much involved in politics as William Brewer. Maud's husband Roger sided with the barons against Henry III in 1258, but afterwards loyally supported Prince Edward, fought for him at Evesham (1265) and Kenilworth (1266), and later against Prince Llywelyn in Wales, where many of his own family estates lay. Roger's grandson, another Roger, fought for Edward I in Gascony and Scotland. Ownership of Bridgwater castle must have been of value when ships and supplies were required for military expeditions. The second Roger and his nephew and namesake tried to build up a power base in Wales which threatened Edward II and his favourites, the Despensers. Both were lodged in the Tower of London in 1322; the nephew escaped in 1324 but the uncle died in custody in 1326. As a precaution the Crown's officers took over Bridgwater castle. Roger the nephew, created Earl of March in 1328, had much influence with Edward II's queen, Isabella, and may well have been responsible for Edward's death. He was hanged for treason in 1330.

The castle ruins. Features of the surviving buildings include a fourteenth-century doorway and sixteenth-century transomed windows. Note the houses in Castle Street. Etching by J. Chubb, *c.* 1800

For the more law-abiding Mortimers the castle was an obviously useful administrative base, and in the 1390s it was noted that cash rents were taken there from the manor of Marshwood in Dorset, on their way to the earl in Wales. The building was said in 1360 to be in ruins, although the castle bailiffs paid for repairs to the chapel and a barn in the 1340s. By that time some of the moat had been filled in and even built over, or was used for grazing the horses which drove the castle mill; but there was still water in the ditch on the town side, for reeds growing in it were cut and used for thatching. In the 1390s a strong oak palisade was rebuilt on the north side; the wall overlooking the river had at least two towers, one at a corner, and both were then repaired. The castle hall, called Mortimer's Hall, had been downgraded to a hay store, but the main entrance from the town was still impressive. It comprised a great outer gate, a drawbridge into the outer bailey, then an inner bridge 'facing the tower within the ditch', and a second drawbridge to the inner bailey.

The castle still bore some semblance of a military stronghold: at least two guns belonged to it and part of its grounds were used for archery practice, but three men had made off with the guns and in 1407 the steward had some difficulty retrieving them. By the 1450s private dwellings had been built within the walls, and it seems likely that the ditch on the town side had long been filled to provide sites for houses and shops on the north side of Fore Street. By 1400 the great days of William Brewer's fortress were long over.

THE NEW TOWN

The town suffered no such decline. King John's charter of 1200 declared it to be a free borough whose leaders, thereafter burgesses, had important legal rights and could trade on privileged terms with others. The lords of the town were able to benefit by levying tolls on outsiders who traded there, while Bridgwater's own traders were able to do business everywhere in the country, except London, toll free. Bridgwater merchants were very soon governing their town, attracting investment, creating and displaying their wealth and making their voices heard in the counsels of the realm.

Among the records of the town is a document sealed with a green wax seal, depicting a three-towered castle with a portcullis guarding its door, the whole placed on a bridge over a river. The surrounding inscription has gone but the document describes the seal as that of the community. Document and seal belong to the middle of the thirteenth century and in it the 'burgesses and community of the borough of Bridgwater', having become a guild and thus able to act together, declare that two of them each year will act as stewards of that guild to ensure that all members followed the rules governing their behaviour towards each other, and particularly that no-one shall attempt to make an unfair profit by buying meat or fish in the borough before 9 a.m.

That declaration was of great importance for the town's future, for although the Mortimers and their fellow lords of the town were still ultimately responsible for law in the borough, the townsmen had taken their first steps towards independence. Only a few records of Mortimer government have survived and date from the end of the fourteenth century, when the borough court met twelve or fourteen times a year – still in their name but in practice administered by the burgesses themselves. By then there were two borough reeves, two bailiffs, two men to ensure that all ale was brewed to the standard strength, two to check on the weight of bread, a janitor for each of the four town gates, and two keepers of the peace for each of the borough's wards or streets.

The Michaelmas law court in October 1378 was particularly busy: twenty people were involved in cases of debt or trespass. John Deye and his servants cut some of the lord's grass without leave; Hugh Goldsmith and his servant took back an animal which the lord's bailiff had confiscated; a dozen men were fined for breaking the peace, for false accusation, or for failing to serve on the jury. The two aletasters had refused to present any brewers, although Thomas Wodelond's ale was so bad it had to be destroyed. A jury of twelve was then sworn, and fined all 195 brewers in the town for breaking the law. Nuisances were also a matter for the court: William Blacche threw skins and cattle horns on the river bank; several left timber and rubbish on the streets; three people had open drains; two choked the town ditch; two were described as 'common scolds and disturbers of the peace'; three tried to raise the price of fish. Fines and deposits payable to the lords of the borough amounted that day to £3 5s 4d and included 14d from a special court called the piepowder court (a corruption of pieds poudreux – for people with dusty feet) which heard cases that arose on market or fair day. There was also another court by the 1370s called the Durneday court which dealt with arrears of rent, and was so called because the door of the property in question would be sealed until the rent was settled.

TRADE

William Brewer's new town depended for success on its ability to attract business, and businessmen needed security, sympathetic government, and space to work and sell. The castle, four sturdy gates to north, south, east and west, and a defensive ditch with some sort of wall at the west side provided security. The merchant guild and the lord's courts were the framework of self-government.

The royal grant to build the castle was accompanied by a licence to hold weekly markets and an annual fair. It seems probable that the early plan of the town provided a large open space under the new castle wall between the church and the river, connected to the new eastern suburb of Eastover by a great stone bridge. Part of William Brewer's royal grant was the right to levy pontage, an indication that the bridge had either just been built or was then planned. By about 1250 the burgesses had assumed responsibility for its maintenance, for the river crossing was vital to their market.

Market day was probably Saturday from 1200 and remained so until the later sixteenth century. The first fair was to last for eight days, beginning on Midsummer Day (24 June). That fair was held each year until about 1359, when no merchants came. For more than a century from 1249 a more popular fair was held for eight days beginning on

Fore Street, once known as
'Twixt Church and Bridge',
showing the cross erected in
1989. The cross is a replica of
one which stood in Penel Orlieu
until the 1830s

The remains of the town's
North Gate, mentioned in 1299
and demolished in 1798

St Matthew's day; and there were two smaller fairs, at Ascension and
Whitsun, but neither lasted much after 1400.

Markets and fairs were presumably held at first in the great market-
place but gradually houses, shops and inns began to encroach on it and
business moved to other parts of the town. There were stalls in the
'great street', later High Street, by the mid-thirteenth century, although
some still stayed in what came to be known as 'twixt church and

Medieval Bridgwater

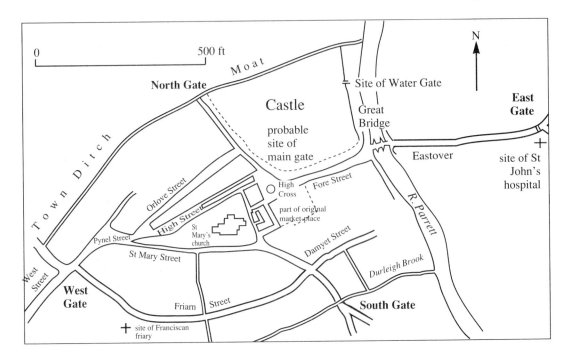

The Cornhill and St Mary's church, *c.* 1800. Timber-framed houses on the site of the present Market House were ripe for improvement. Etching by J. Chubb

bridge', now Fore Street; and the corn merchants remained at the west end of the original market-place, which came to be known as Cornchepyng or Cornhill. Butchers and fishmongers were to be found with other tradesmen in the warren of temporary stalls in High Street, forming alleys such as Cokenrewe and Chapman Row, which indicated the business of the traders there. By 1367 a market hall sheltered some of the traders, and a tolsey was established where rents for stalls were paid. By about the same date the pillared High Cross sheltered some of the corn merchants.

Cattle were usually sold in a triangular area called le Orfaire, just inside the west gate. St Matthew's fair, for which there was evidently no room in the town, was moved to the field just outside the west gate by 1404 and has been held there ever since.

In 1249 Roger Mortimer received the rents of burgages (town houses), shops and stalls, the tolls from markets, fairs and the quay, and the profits from the courts of law amounting to £13 5s 6d, about two-thirds of the value of his share of the whole estate. By 1257 there were more than 300 town houses, thirteen stalls and five shops in his possession.

St Matthew's Fair, 1956: combining business with pleasure

Penel Orlieu and the old cross, 1850. The artist, W.W. Wheatley, noted that the cross had been pulled down '25 years since'

Markets and fairs, of course, attracted buyers and sellers from outside the town, some of whom began to settle. In a deed dated 1245 William of Ferndone (possibly Farringdon in North Petherton) made over half a house, a shop and a yard. The agreement was witnessed by several people including Robert Dorchester, William of Enmore and Walter of Kentisbere, presumably a native of East Devon. Other deeds from the same date record the names of people from near and far: Robert of Coker, William of Evercreech, John of Axbridge (a goldsmith), Henry of Goathurst, William of Sticklepath, Eustace of Hemyock, all from Somerset or neighbouring counties; but also Walter the Irishman, John the Welshman, and perhaps another foreigner, Walter Ordlof, from whom the Orlieu in Penel Orlieu comes.

There were two other sure signs of prosperity. One was a small community of Jews who acted as bankers for the merchants: in 1256–7 Bateman the Jew was licensed to stay in the town for a year, Mampson the Jew for part of the year and Koket the Jew was fined for a trespass. And the Church was another canny investor. William Brewer gave St John's hospital its land outside the town and also gave his favourite Abbey of Dunkeswell a property inside. Muchelney Abbey and Taunton Priory both had houses in High Street, Athelney Abbey several houses, and an inn called the Saracen's Head. More significant was the Franciscan friary, founded in 1245-6 and by 1358 moved to a site between the town ditch and the Durleigh brook to make way for some new burgages. A friary is a sure sign of good business.

Friarn Street, so named after the Franciscan Friary founded in the town 1245–6, and moved to a site outside the town boundary by 1358. It was photographed *c*. 1907

THE PORT

It is not easy to assess the value of Bridgwater as a port before 1400 because the accounts of customs paid there were included with those of Bristol. Certainly, about 1300 the lords of Bridgwater received more cash from market tolls than from the port, but at the same time Bridgwater merchants had begun trading in wine with Bordeaux, and in the 1340s Florentine bankers were using the port as a collecting point for their wool exports. Men like David le Palmer, Hugh le Mareys, John Michel and John Cole shipped large quantities of corn, beans and peas to Ireland, southern France and northern Spain, and a few tried to evade customs by loading hides and wool fells in the river, or by using creeks like Combwich to send corn to Ireland without licence.

Most merchants were presumably law-abiding and contributed to the town's coffers. In the year from Michaelmas 1396 Richard Salter, the bailiff of the community, accounted for 18*s* received from rents of houses in the town, 33*s* 11*d* from a local tax and 56*s* 7*d* from 'issues of the bridge', that is from the port, and comprising money for hiring out ropes and skids for dragging barrels along the quay to the town cellar and other sums for using planks and the bushel measure. One of the planks, broken by a stranger who was charged 8*d*, was sold for 10*d*. A special device made in that year was a wooden gangway strong enough for unloading stone or tuns of wine. Two years later the total port income had risen to 122*s*, which included a charge for hauling 101 tuns of wine. The new gangway had been a sound investment.

THE PARISH CHURCH

Such prosperity had its outward show. John de Mulle, who died in 1310, left his best brass plate and jar to his wife, his second best to his daughter, several yards of cloth each to them, to his son, his brother, his sister and others, and cash to each of his godchildren. Roger Sopham (d. 1361) left over £44 in cash and money to build a causeway between Bridgwater and Horsey. Robert Plympton had so much property in and around the town, including a tavern in High Street, that his will, which has not survived, had to be proved in the bishop's consistory court after his death in 1376. No doubt Plympton would have been as much concerned for his immortal soul as were Sopham and Mulle; Mulle left money to the parish church, to all its clergy – vicar, parish and other chaplains, the deacon and two other clerks – and cash to maintain a light on the Lady altar.

By 1400 St Mary's church, not quite as large as now, had a staff of at least eight clergymen serving the high altar and altars of the Blessed Virgin, All Saints and St Catherine, and lights or images before the

St Mary's church from the south-east, showing the crenellated parapet and curious bay window beside the south door. Wash drawing by J. Buckler, 1828

rood and elsewhere. The church itself, already aisled by the early thirteenth century, was extended west and given transepts in the fourteenth century. Major rebuilding work cost over £140 in 1366–7, a sum raised largely by loans and gifts collected throughout the parish. The work seems to have been on the tower, and most of the cash was paid to Nicholas Waleys, a well-known Bristol mason. The tower was apparently still unfinished in 1385.

TOWNSMEN

The whole building, full of colour and light, was the spiritual home of a community which by 1377 totalled some 858 people, the second Somerset town after Wells. The voice of such a town needed to be heard beyond the county. John atte Weye and Walter Jacob were the first men to be chosen when they attended the parliament of 1295, and from 1298 the borough sent two men to every parliament until the 1860s. During the fourteenth century many of them seem to have come from outside the town, and more than half do not appear in local records; but some were prominent local men like Richard of Sticklepath, Walter Fychet, David le Palmer, John Saladyn and Robert Plympton, men who could speak for their community. Perhaps the most prominent of all was William Thomere, deputy for the Admiral in the West and steward of the town's guild merchant, who served in fourteen parliaments between 1377 and 1406. Two others may be noted. John Fittleton, chosen in 1380, was a local landowner employed by the Earl of March; the earl may well have found his voice useful in the Commons house. The other was Thomas Engelby, chosen in 1368. He regularly appeared as a witness to title deeds in the town in the following decade, but it was as leader of the insurrection in 1381 that he brought Bridgwater some national notoriety.

Three times in 1380 a crowd of people appeared at St John's hospital led by a group of prominent townsmen like the tanner William Blacche, Richard Salter, Hugh Mareys, John Sopham and, on the last occasion, William Thomere, William Tannere, and Thomas Engelby. Exactly what was the trouble is not certain, but the hospital was owed all the tithes of the parish, appointed the vicar, and had some sort of hold over the townsmen in the form of bonds either for their good behaviour or for debts they owed. The Zouche family were also unhappy because the hospital's servants had tried to prevent them from holding courts.

Only a week after Wat Tyler was killed at Smithfield and the burgesses of St Albans had attacked the abbot there, in what was later

All that remained above ground
of St John's hospital, re-erected
in Monmouth street

known as the Peasants' Revolt, Thomas Engelby and Nicholas
Frampton, the vicar, led a mob from the Cornhill to the gates of the
hospital, and forced the master to hand over the offending bonds, to
promise to pay the vicar his proper wages, and to give them 200 marks
in cash.

The mob then turned on two lawyers, John Sydenham and Thomas
Duffield, damaged their houses and stole legal documents; and after
that went off to the county gaol at Ilchester, where they dragged the
former keeper from one of his own cells, and brought back his head
for exhibition on the great bridge.

Within a year or so even Thomas Engelby was pardoned, and the
last heard of him was when he was fined 1*d* in the borough court in
1387 for leaving rubbish outside his door. Among the other offenders
at the same court was William Blacche, who had washed skins in the
stream at the bottom of his garden, the same stream which his neigh-
bours used for their domestic water supply.

CHAPTER THREE

Power and Prosperity, 1400–1530

T he account of Richard Baker, bailiff of the community from Michaelmas 1399 to Michaelmas 1400, was written on paper; not the first paper used in Bridgwater, but the first with a watermark. The drawn bow within a circle suggests that it was made in Piedmont and probably came from Genoa. By 1400 Bridgwater had become a port of significance and from 1402 it was separated from Bristol. Henceforward

The Parrett flows out to sea.
Brent Knoll is in the distance

customs officers were based in the port, and had jurisdiction which included the Parrett and the coast between the Axe at Brean Down and Watchet.

TRADE

In 1410 one of the town's most prosperous merchants, John Kedwelly, presented a petition to parliament. He complained that his little boat the *Cog John* went to La Rochelle for wine. Despite a truce between England and France the men of Harfleur seized the crew and cargo and demanded £200. Harfleur and St Malo men had also taken another of his boats and sold its cargo to some Spaniards. Two of his men and sixty pieces of cloth were held in Cherbourg.

Trading on the high seas had serious dangers, but Bridgwater merchants were prepared to take the risk, and exporting cloth and importing wine was for more than a century its most important business. Most of the cloth was probably produced in Somerset and Devon, although some came from Wales and Ireland to be finished and dyed in the town. Before the end of the fourteenth century Taunton 'straits', Barnstaple 'dozens', and Bridgwater 'straits', 'osetts' and 'dozens' were being sent to Andalusia, and the same kinds of cloth at the end of the fifteenth century were taken regularly to Bordeaux and Bayonne in south-western France and to San Sebastian, Bilbao and Fuenterrabia in northern Spain. At the same time boats like the *Marie* of Tintern were bringing in via Bristol undyed Welsh flannel, and other coarse cloth came from Ireland along with wool to be processed by local craftsmen. The importance of cloth exports to Bridgwater will be obvious from the following table:

Cloths Exported from Bridgwater, 1410–1530

1410–20	921	1470–80	2435
1420–30	775	1480–90	4690
1430–40	746	1490–1500	4958
1440–50	873	1500–10	4115
1450–60	892	1510–20	2603
1460–70	304*	1520–30	2067

* Some customs accounts missing.

Source: *England's Export Trade, 1275–1547*, ed. E.M. Carus Wilson and Olive Coleman (1963), pp. 88–119.

The medieval Town Bridge and the Langport Slip. Etching by J. Chubb, *c.* 1800

In return came wine, woad for dyeing cloth, and iron. Amounts of wine varied from year to year: none, for instance, in 1470 but 366 tuns in 1475–6, each tun containing 252 gallons. The average amount each year was about 102 tuns (25,704 gallons). In 1504–5 just over 285 tuns were unloaded, including small amounts of sweet white wine but mostly the dry wine from La Rochelle, the Bordeaux region, Portugal and southern Spain.

A good deal of business was done with the Bristol Channel ports and with Ireland. Farm produce, usually beans, went to Ireland, and often in return came fish such as red herring, salmon and conger eels, hides and sometimes empty barrels. Coastal trade stretched around the south-west peninsula as far as Melcombe Regis and might, of course, have led to longer voyages. John Couper, for instance, was licensed in 1485 to take the *George* of Bridgwater to Bordeaux with 100 'fothers' of tin, presumably from Cornwall, and to return to his home port with wine.

The town benefited in different ways from this trade. Goods coming in were unloaded with the help of the town's crane and gangplanks, measured with the town's bushel and stored in the town's cellar and were subject to small charges which brought in a modest £5 or £6 a year in the 1420s, but £20 by the end of the century. There was also money to be made carrying goods inland: up the Parrett from the New Slip (later called the Langport Slip) and still to be seen at Binford Place; or by cart and horseback along roads in every direction.

By the end of the fifteenth century Bridgwater's merchants were doing well. One of the most successful was John Hill (d. 1481) who left shares in the *Margaret*, the *John* and the *Nicholas*, and gave away in his will large quantities of woad. Another was Denis Dwyn, an Irishman but also a burgess and former bailiff of the town, who traded with Bordeaux in woad, cloth and wine in his ship the *Gabriel*, and who at his death in 1504 had business connections with merchants in Cherbourg, Limerick, Langport and probably Stow on the Wold. Not long before his death a fellow Irishman took him to court for failing to pay for some cod with which he had victualled his ship on its way back from Bordeaux; his business at Limerick was to exchange French wine for Atlantic whiting.

Perhaps the most successful merchant of his time was John Kendall, probably a native of Taunton but almost certainly Bridgwater's first mayor in 1468 and probably three times more; MP for the borough certainly three times and probably six; deputy butler in the port from 1478 and merchant banker as well as general trader, who did business with men of London, Melcombe Regis, Bristol, Southampton, Exeter,

Wells and Bordeaux. And, of course, a generous benefactor not only to his parish church but also to the friars of Bridgwater and Ilchester.

GOVERNING THE TOWN

At the beginning of 1467 the sum of £1 2*s* 8*d* was paid to Kendall, then the borough's MP, 'for the renewal of our common charter'. Ever since 1200, when William Brewer had been given a charter by King John to develop his new town, the people had been gradually taking charge of their own affairs. Together they had bought property in the name of their community, and in practice they had long been administering the town's courts.

Now in 1468, thanks evidently to the efforts of Kendall and others of influence, the king granted a charter which gave Bridgwater complete self-government. Instead of two common stewards appointed each year who were obliged to account to the Zouches and the Duchess of York as lords of the castle and borough, the town became a corporation comprising a mayor and probably twenty burgesses (the charter did not actually mention the number); a small group which hardly increased in number and for nearly four centuries governed the town. Each year on 8 September, according to the charter, the burgesses were to choose a mayor to preside over their deliberations and a recorder to give them legal advice. They also appointed a town clerk to keep their records, and later two water bailiffs to collect the port charges.

Charter Day service, St Mary's church, June 1950

All these changes were, declared the charter, 'for the sound and wholesome government' of the town, and government included administering law and order. Every Monday the mayor and bailiffs held the borough court to ensure fair trading and good behaviour, and the mayor and the recorder held quarterly sessions for more serious offences. Only a small cash payment was a reminder of the past: each year the corporation was to pay £3 to the Duchess of York and £6 to the Zouches.

The first mayor, John Kendall, seems to have been a relative newcomer. His successors like Adam Hamlyn, William Michell and John Cosyn could look back over many years of service to the town. Hamlyn had been one of the last stewards of the community and had first taken office in 1460–1. In that year, rents of houses and shops belonging to the town brought in 46s 3½d, the port charges produced 24s 2d, and debts recovered 33s 4d, making a total of 103s 9½d. Expenditure included costs of property repairs, of erecting chains and other barriers on the great bridge, maintenance of the crane and 5s paid to the craneman for scouring the river bank for 'slyme' below the quay. Hamlyn would perhaps still remember the unusual charges: the visit of Humphrey Stafford, lord of Southwick, which cost 7s 10d in bread, ale, chicken and other food; and the 3 gallons 3 quarts of wine given to the master of St John's hospital and the friars on Corpus Christi day.

Two or three years earlier, income and expenditure were very much the same, always including some charge for Corpus Christi day and presents for high and mighty visitors such as the Duchess of Exeter, Duchess Cecily's daughter, who was given some wine in 1456–7 and two oxen in the following year. In 1458 the abbot of Glastonbury came on the feast of the Assumption and the town built a canopy in the churchyard for him and gave him a meal. There had probably been much excitement in 1431–2 when a play was performed in the shire hall, and again in 1449 when the pipers from Ash Priors took part in the annual Corpus Christi pageant. This pageant, sometimes called the shepherds' pageant, took place regularly until 1543. The king's players visited the town in 1461–2.

Very little had changed by the end of the fifteenth century, although by 1494–5 the town accounts were in two parts, the water bailiff being charged to collect port dues and to pay the fees of the mayor, the recorder and the town clerk. He also paid for repairs, gifts to visiting minstrels from Bristol and from royal and noble households, for the Corpus Christi pageant, and for a feast given to the Lord Chamberlain, Lord Daubeney, then both constable of the castle and temporary possessor of the Zouche share in the borough and manor. John Pery of

Huntworth brought a buck for the feast from Petherton park, Clement of Haygrove made it into 'pasteys' and an unnamed baker was given 4*d* for baking them.

THE PARISH CHURCH

St Mary's church from the north-east, showing perpendicular tracery in most of the windows. Wash drawing by J.C. Buckler, 1828

To the merchants and craftsmen of the town, lavish spending on their church was natural, and probably for almost a century major works were going forward somewhere in the building. The chancel was the first to be rebuilt, or at least re-roofed, presumably by St John's hospital as rector, for a boss there bears the initials WC for William Camel, master of the hospital between 1385 and 1416. The church-wardens then turned their attention to the north transept where three chapels were created in the few years before 1418, as well as the great rood screen. Then came work on the nave about 1420 and, after a pause, more work in the 1440s including the extension of the chancel and the creation of another chapel.

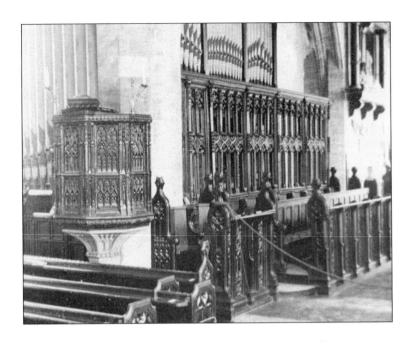

St Mary's church, *c.* 1910: medieval pulpit and screen after W.H. Brakspear's restoration

Robert Crosse and John Staulynch, churchwardens in 1414–15, raised £20 from collections in the parish and 22*s* 6*d* in gifts. Most of the money was spent on finishing Holy Cross and Holy Trinity chapels, and on repairing the Lady chapel with stone brought by river from Pibsbury beyond Langport, recasting the great bell, and repaying debts to the town and to a merchant. Other items included preparing timber for the new rood screen, parts of which still survive behind the choir stalls, and paying 1*d* to a man for drawing up a contract with Philip Mason to build St Anne's chapel.

Three years later the Easter collection raised only 8*s* out of total receipts of just over £4. The wardens bought two great oak trees to complete the rood screen which cost nearly half the money they raised; 9*s* 6*d* went on the Easter candle and 2*s* on painting the picture of the Resurrection. Wine was given to the chaplain preparing the Easter Sepulchre for Corpus Christi day and 8*d* for repairing the cross used for Sunday processions.

By Michaelmas 1420 the great screen, made up by carpenters in a lodge in the churchyard, was fixed by masons who bored holes in the pillars. They and the carpenters took a week putting it in place. John Outremer and William Thomas fixed the old rood beam above it. In that year the wardens bought plain and striped silk ribbons and muslin to dress the images of saints, Thomas Phelpis made colours for the screen, a silver censer and service books were repaired, and linen cloth was bought for amices. The wardens overspent by nearly £4.

From the mid-fifteenth century there are records of how the parishioners contributed to repairs and new work each year. In 1444–5 money was raised from 354 people within the town; and in 1447–8 the collectors produced nearly £12, made up to over £20 from gifts and the sale of old timber and lead. In that year there was work on the chapels of Our Lady and St George.

By 1450 the church employed nine other priests besides the vicar, John Colswayn, including John Wheler the parish chaplain, one priest serving the chantry of the Virgin, and the rest saying anniversary masses. People continued to give generously to ensure the safety of their souls. John Colswayn himself wanted a memorable funeral, leaving money to every priest and clerk who attended, and a small sum to the bellringers and the bedeman. Much larger sums were to go to the mayor and the organist, and there was provision for bread, ale, wine and spices for the funeral feast and for a perpetual endowment for tapers to burn before the high altar.

In the 1480s the chantry chapels each had their own property and wardens. St Catherine's chapel, the best endowed, had a magnificent collection of vestments of many colours and materials including silk and damask, altar cloths, banners, candlesticks, plate and bells. Some people left property for their masses, some cash. Agnes Cutler gave her late husband's anvil, to be shared between the chapels of St Catherine and St Erasmus; Agnes Trowte gave a pair of tucker's shears to be hired out. John Kendall was typical of his class. He died in 1489 and wished to be buried in St George's chapel, to which he gave a house and a butcher's stall for the salary of a priest. Most of his property went to his widow for her life, but three properties in the town were to go to the guild of St Anne for a requiem mass, to be sung at the altar of St George every four years. Thus a man might secure a safer course to heaven and remind his fellow townsmen of his name and earthly success.

FRIENDS AT COURT

The new charter declared Saturday to be market day (as it probably had been for years) and revived the old Ascension Day fair which was moved to the five days beginning on the Monday after Shrove Tuesday. This was, presumably, a move to stimulate trade. In 1454 the burgesses had complained that their income was damaged by taxation, and in appealing for the new charter they declared that the town 'have ben fall in so grete poverte and decaye' that some people had left and they could not find the rent they owed to the lords of the town. Their

West Street on Fair Day, 1954

cry was heard and the Duchess of York offered a substantial reduction. But was this a reward for political loyalty, perhaps the result of having friends at Court?

The town was, after all, a Yorkist possession. Until 1460 its castle belonged to Richard Plantagenet, Duke of York, leader of the opposition to the weak government of Henry VI, and after Henry's defeat his acknowledged successor until his own death at Wakefield. His widow held the castle and his share in the borough and Haygrove manor. William, Lord Zouche, was nominal lord of the rest of the town and manor. He was thought of as a supporter by Henry VI's government in 1459–60, and his son and namesake, succeeding in 1462, secured a royal pardon, a sensible precaution whatever opinions he held.

But both lords were remote from the town and the leaders of Bridgwater cannot be said to have been either Lancastrian or Yorkist. In 1449 they chose a member of Henry VI's household, Thomas Driffield, as one of their MPs. Their permanent legal counsel,

Alexander Hody, of West Bower and Gothelney, was another active Lancastrian who fought against York at Wakefield with a group of his own tenants and went on with them to St Albans. He probably also fought at Towton, and died attainted a few days afterwards.

The county sent Humphrey Stafford to Edward IV's first parliament, a young Yorkist then living at Enmore, who shortly after his election was chosen to serve as sheriff. He was knighted after the Yorkist victory at Towton and soon afterwards was summoned to the House of Lords as Lord Stafford of Southwick. In 1465 the king appointed him constable of Bridgwater castle, steward of the lordship and manor of Bridgwater, and keeper of Petherton forest. The bailiff and burgesses entertained him several times – it was the politic thing to do, for he was a powerful, if increasingly unpopular, figure.

In 1468 Stafford was involved with the judicial murder of two leading Lancastrians, and soon afterwards was given the earldom of Devon, to which one of the victims had been heir. As opposition to Edward IV grew, Stafford led troops from the west towards Nottingham in answer to the king's summons. The other half of the royal army was defeated at Edgecote near Banbury, and Stafford fled with a price on his head, offered in the name of the king but in fact by Stafford's enemy Warwick the Kingmaker.

Stafford returned, by now evidently a prisoner, to Bridgwater. There, probably in the castle, he completed his long will 'writen [by] my hande the day of my dethe'. Later the Nevilles let it be known that he had been beheaded on 17 August 1469 in Bridgwater 'by the commons'. The will shows how wrong that was. He was executed on Neville instructions. The town which had achieved self-government a year earlier, probably with his help, did not betray him. John Kendall acted as his loyal executor.

It is possible that Bridgwater was involved in national affairs again in 1483, in the rebellion against Richard III which is associated with the Duke of Buckingham. One of the conspirators was Sir Giles Daubeney, whom Edward IV had appointed constable of the castle. Failure of risings in Wales and the south-east allowed Richard to move into Dorset and then Devon, thus thwarting the planned landing of Henry Tudor from France. Were these the 'daily coming and going of military carts' which in 1484–5 were declared to be part of the reason why money was needed to repair the great bridge?

A large force certainly came through the town in 1497. It had started in Cornwall, formed in opposition to extra taxation, and came across the great bridge on the way to Wells and defeat at Blackheath outside London. Thirty-seven Bridgwater people were fined a total of £166, of which Denis Dwyn and Walter Manne of Fore Street and John Baker of Friarn Street had to find £20 each. Dunwear, Pignes, Horsey and Hamp produced a further sixty-five sympathizers. No further trouble is known until 1528, when justices of the peace found themselves unable to hold their courts because of an insurrection which also involved Taunton.

CHAPTER FOUR

Tudor Problems, 1530–1600

THE PORT

T he decline of cloth exports from Bridgwater after about 1510 had a serious effect on the town as a whole, and instead of the average of about £20 a year coming into the town coffers from port charges, only about half as much came in the 1530s and early 1540s. From the 1550s, however, income rose to over £25 in most years because of the success of the millstone monopoly. The number of ships belonging to the port during the same period was remarkably small: only five in 1508–9 and, according to a survey of 1570, only one, the *Jhesus*, was actually in port, 'the residue of the shippes there being but fewe in number and now beyonde the seas'. Two years later another survey found the *Brave* in port and a total of seven with a combined tonnage of 136 tons. Yet trade as a whole was said to be increasing in the 1560s and Bridgwater was the largest port in Somerset. A slump in the late 1580s and 1590s found only one ship of any size belonging to the port, and the collector of customs complained that in 1596 there was so little trade he had not collected enough to cover his fees.

In the 1540s and 1550s cloth was still leaving for traditional destinations, and the corporation went to considerable expense in 1555 to obtain an Act of Parliament to ensure the size and quality of the 'Bridgwaters', 'Tauntons' and 'Chards' that went through the port. Four ships leaving in the last quarter of 1547 took between them fifty-one 'serges', thirty-four-dozen 'kerseys' and thirty-two dozen 'Tauntons'.

The other important export was agricultural produce, mostly beans, especially when corn was dear overseas. Most went to Ireland: in 1571 the port was one of the official places from which grain, butter and cheese could be sent. Hides were also exported: ninety-four dozen calfskins went to San Sebastian at the end of 1547.

The hazards of the Parrett,
photographed in 1938

Just occasionally a more exotic ship or cargo found its way into the Parrett. A Venetian ship foundered on the Huntspill bank in 1548 and two local graziers, normally making a living from fattening cattle, undertook to remove the hull from the mud since it was a danger to shipping. In 1563 the mayor took custody of a cargo of coarse canvas sailcloth called poldavy, valued at nearly £58, owned by a company of Antwerp merchants. At the end of the century two captains had some trouble with the customs in Bristol, and brought their cargoes of Canary Island sugar into Bridgwater instead.

Local trade with the Bristol Channel ports was now of growing importance although it is difficult to judge its volume. For a time in the 1560s and 1570s the corporation had a monopoly in the purchase and resale of millstones from the Forest of Dean. At the end of 1572, for instance, there were thirty-eight millstones, forty-five grindstones, nineteen corn stones, four mustard mills and a horsemill stone stacked on the quay, awaiting sale and removal as far away as the Dorset coast and well into Devon. As many as seventy-six stones were sold in 1590–1.

Welsh timber, iron and coal were also imported, not just for local consumption but for buyers inland. Welsh boards bought at the port were made into a roodloft for the village church at Trull about 1536. By the 1580s iron was arriving from an estate of Sir William Herbert and in 1601–2 the *George* of Newport and the *Peter*, the *Andrew* and the *Griffin* of Cardiff between them brought 122 tons of iron and 2 'wayes' of coal, which were loaded into barges called 'lytteres' to be taken under the great bridge and up the Parrett and Tone to a valued customer, Alexander Hill of Taunton. In another year – when Thomas Beard was water bailiff – Hill took 80 tons of iron and 5 'wayes' of coal, and thus owed, according to the craneman at Bridgwater, 14*s* 2*d* in charges.

During the sixteenth century there were no merchants in the town to match John Kedwelly or John Kendall, although John Hill was involved in the Gascon wine trade in the 1540s. Men such as Richard Castleman, John Newport or Robert and John Hamond seem to have left the risks of shipping to others. In the 1530s and 1540s one of those others was John Smythe of Bristol, who had been apprenticed in Bridgwater in the 1520s either to Thomas Hoper or to Simon White. He married Simon's widow after 1529. Smythe had regular customers in the town: Robert Bishop, Robert and John Hamond, John a Wood, Jeffry Arundell and John Gibbs, landlord of the Saracen's Head. Gibbs, naturally, bought wine: sack (from Spain), bastard and ossey (from Portugal), claret (from Gascony). Robert Bishop bought muscadel, sack, claret and bastard; John Hamond sack, Gascon wine, olive oil, and woad from the Azores. John a Wood, a fuller, bought woad from Toulouse.

THE REFORMATION

From 1528 until 1557 Thomas Strete was vicar of St Mary's, a period of great change in the life of the Church in the town. He had been here ten years when John Herys, warden of the Franciscan friars, and his six brethren left their house for the last time. A year later Robert Walshe and his seven fellow canons surrendered St John's hospital to the officers of the king. By that time Hamp manor no longer belonged to Athelney Abbey, for that, too, had been surrendered; and by the end of 1539 all the other monastic property in the town including the Saracen's Head inn, also belonged to the Crown and was on the market.

These changes hardly affected the clergy at St Mary's, but there were more to come. In 1548 a government survey found that the parish was in the care of Vicar Strete, and there was an assistant priest whose Sunday duty was to say Mass in Horsey chapel. In addition there were three other priests based at the parish church who served the chantries of St George, Our Lady and the Trinity. The chantries were dissolved in accordance with the new policy of the government that praying for the dead served no purpose; and at the same time other small endowments for prayers for the dead and for permanent lights were confiscated.

Other changes are less easy to trace in Bridgwater, though in most places the rood was torn down as idolatrous, stone altars were removed when the Mass was abandoned, images were smashed, sacred vessels sold and clergy scattered. At St Mary's there seems to have been compliance with the letter of the law, but a determination to change little. John Newport and John Watts had evidently bought chalices and other plate to the enormous value of £132 when the Mass was replaced by the simpler communion service, but found themselves in trouble when Queen Mary restored the Mass and it was required again in 1554. In 1557 a 22 oz. chalice was still missing. The three ex-chantry priests were still working in the church in 1551, and in 1554 the corporation bought some of the former chantry property with the specific objects (laid down by the queen's government) of finding priests to 'help the vicar in the services' and of endowing a perpetual mass. At the time of Strete's death in 1557, prayers were being said again for the dead.

In 1561 the mayor and corporation bought some of the property formerly belonging to St John's hospital, including the great tithes of the parish, but in return were supposed to employ two priests to serve the church. However, for several years there was no vicar, and the parish clerk sometimes found himself burying the dead. Among the preachers who stayed for only a few months was John Bullingham, who was also vicar of Creech St Michael and was later to become bishop of Gloucester and Bristol. From 1571 the corporation undertook to pay £20 a year for a man to teach and preach in the town and neighbourhood and £13 6s 8d for a curate. They were also to find a schoolmaster. By the end of the century and until the 1630s the vicar's income was still so small that he also took one of the other posts. But by that time religious attitudes seem to have changed. The corporation which had publicly rejoiced at the news that Mary Tudor was expecting a child, thus ensuring the future for traditional Catholicism, was now ready to ensure the success of the Elizabethan Settlement.

Mansion House Lane, c. 1907, named after the inn at the junction with High Street. The Church House, on the site by 1537, housed the grammar school by 1722

THE TOWN AND THE NATION

The demand for English cloth which brought so much business to the port at the turn of the sixteenth century is better reflected in the church towers of the wool-producing villages than in Bridgwater. John Leland, visiting the town about 1540, heard that more than 200 houses had fallen into decay in living memory, and a survey of 1563 found only 352 households in the parish as compared with a population of about 1,600 in the 1440s.

The castle, as Leland also noted, was 'all going to mere ruin', and part of it fell down and was used to build a house for the port's customs collector. Other parts provided a site for a customs house and a new quay. Property taken from the dissolved monasteries and chantries reduced rent values, and when no buyers could be found the town was 'at the point of utter ruin'. The corporation, which had bought some of the houses, was faced with heavy repair bills and could find no tenants. In 1558 repairs and lost rents cost more than income, and the corporation had to borrow heavily from its own members.

Outside the town farming was undergoing change, but in a period of severe inflation was also in difficulty. There were probably no common arable fields in the east of the parish by the sixteenth century, although traces of them could still be found at Hamp, Slape Cross, Horsey and Dunwear. Improved farming practice allowed the farmers in the area to produce nearly three-quarters of the corn grown in the parish. The less efficient strip system was still in use in North Field,

Part of the castle, 1792

Farmer's Corner, Monmouth Street: the town's agricultural past still lingered in 1957

Matthew's Field and Hayle Field, north and east of the town. Everywhere farms were small and mainly for subsistence. Hamp manor, where grassland was becoming more important than arable, had been bought by the corporation of Bristol after Athelney Abbey had been dissolved, and amounted to about 620 acres. The land was shared between more than fifty little farms, most of which were of 20 acres or less. Yet Hamp was the scene of one splendid piece of enterprise. In 1568 Bristol corporation undertook to make a new channel for the river in order to improve its flow, and organized a vast labour force drawn from villages across the Levels.

Despite its economic difficulties, Bridgwater remained a town of significance, but men chosen for parliament were usually connected with the port rather than the town. The two members for the important 1529 parliament, Henry Thornton and Hugh Trotter, both had land not far away but also held office in the port. Sir Thomas Dyer, a royal household official, was chosen as MP five times, but throughout the reign of Elizabeth the Pophams of Huntworth dominated the local

A sixteenth-century fragment in Silver Street: a doorway has become a shop window

political scene from their powerful position as recorders of the corporation. The 'potell' of sack drunk by Master Popham and Master Dyer at Master Arundell's house over dinner after the sessions in November 1543 was a proper recognition of their power.

And as in the fifteenth century, so in the sixteenth the town needed friends. In 1525–6 the water bailiff bought a gallon of wine for the Lord Chief Justice; in 1540–1 a quart of wine was given to Master Portman 'when the subsidy was set', no doubt to influence him in the town's favour; in the same year a gallon was produced for the Earl of Bath's visit; in 1543–4 a 'potell' of wine for the Bishop of Bath. Apparently much more expensive were the minstrels and players, who regularly visited the town; perhaps the size of their rewards was an indication of the political value of their patron. In 1540–1 the Earl of Bridgwater's players received 5s for performing at the mayor's house and the Earl of Bath's 2s even though they did not play. In 1543–4 the Marquess of Dorset's players received 6s, the Earl of Bath's 2s 4d. At other times there were visits from the king's minstrels and the players of the Duke of Somerset, the Earl of Worcester and the Lord Admiral. In 1543 there was evidently a humbler group led by one Gybbys, who played at the mayor's house 'yn Cryssmas hollydayes' and received 2s 8d.

There were, of course, other excitements, notably the bonfire on the Cornhill when a rumour reached the town that Queen Mary was pregnant; the annual visit of Harry the bearward in the 1540s; and the normal disturbances to be expected every fair day which meant a special guard on the town hall. Two events far from the town proved of local importance. The first was the loss of Calais in 1557. The government demanded soldiers, weapons and money; Bridgwater obliged with £8 19s in cash, of which the members of the corporation raised rather more than half. They also produced a mass of bills, swords, daggers, bows and arrows, poleaxes and suits of armour. Mr Boyes, the mayor, Mr Newport, Mr Watkyns and Mr Moleyns led the way, each offering 6s 8d , a 'pair of harnesses', a bill, bow and sheaf of arrows.

The second was the threat of war with Spain early in 1569. Each county was to have men in readiness at the muster, and volunteers or not, the borough produced seventeen billmen, six pikemen, seventeen archers and three gunners, and Horsey, Hamp, Dunwear and East Bower between them a further eighteen billmen, five pikemen and six archers. As in the earlier crisis, arms and armour were again needed and the borough and its leaders, including Mr Boyes and Mr Moleyns, produced five small cannon called arquebuses, six suits of armour and weapons for a pikeman, and nine suits and weapons for a light pikeman.

Spain continued to be a threat, and by 1586 there were lookout towers and cannon at strategic points on the Channel coast and a gun at Combwich. In April 1588 Bridgwater was ordered to produce a ship and a pinnace, complete with crews and supplies for the royal fleet, then in preparation. The *William*, 70 tons, and presumably the pinnace, joined Drake's division at Plymouth under the command of Captain John Smyth, and later served under the Lord Admiral, Lord Howard of Effingham. Bridgwater corporation demonstrated their loyalty by offering more stores than the government requested. Command of the sea was, after all, in the interest of Bridgwater merchants.

CHAPTER FIVE

The Age of Robert Blake, 1600–1660

Robert Blake was born in 1598 in the family home in Blake Street, which now houses the town's museum. His father Humphrey (d. 1625), a successful merchant, sent him to the town's grammar school, which could trace its origins back to the late thirteenth century in St John's hospital and which now was supported by the corporation.

Robert Blake, Bridgwater's favourite son, from the portrait at Wadham College, Oxford

He was sent to Wadham College, Oxford, at the age of sixteen and may well have joined the family business. At the age of forty-two in 1640 he was chosen as one of the two men sent by his native town to what was to be famous as the Short Parliament, so called because the king dissolved it rather than agree to the demands of its members (led by John Pym from nearby Brymore in Cannington) to discuss grievances before voting taxation. Blake was not chosen for the next parliament, called later in the same year; his place was taken by a country gentleman, Edmund Wyndham of Kentsford, later to be royalist governor of the town during the Civil War. Perhaps already Blake had made himself unacceptable by committing himself to the cause of parliamentary liberty.

In electing Blake in 1640 the corporation had chosen a member of the town's merchant community for the first time since 1604. For nearly forty years local gentry – Halswells, Warres and Pophams – had held office as the town's recorder, its chief legal adviser, and had influenced every election. But a slight change had come about in 1628 when a new charter increased the number of capital burgesses, the electorate, from eighteen to twenty-four. These new men, the choice of the existing mayor and aldermen, increased the voice of the local merchant. The immediate result was not dramatic: the men chosen in that year for parliament were gentry – Sir Thomas Wroth of Petherton Park and Thomas Smythe of Long Ashton. But Wroth, also just appointed the town's recorder, was certainly an independent political voice; and

Blake Bridge under
construction, 1957

Smythe, only eighteen years old and hoping to be chosen again, sent
the mayor a buck from his estate for a feast. He lost to Blake in the
first election of 1640 but later replaced Edmund Wyndham, and was
considered radical by many of the county's politicians. Bridgwater
was thus in 1640 represented at a critical time by two gentlemen less
than sympathetic to the king's cause.

There is a strong suspicion that Bridgwater was also radical in matters of religion. In John Devenish, vicar from 1605, the corporation
found a man of puritan sympathies. George Swankin, preacher by
1595 until 1622, and his successor George Wootton, had similar
views. For these men, preaching was of the greatest importance, and
the corporation demonstrated their public support by installing their
own seats in the parish church. These seats were not then tucked away
in the south transept but were placed in front of the screen, facing
west. For both clergy and people the parish church had become a
preaching house, dominated by the pulpit which stood high on the
north side of the nave.

Such practices ran counter to the views of Charles I, Archbishop
Laud of Canterbury, and Bishop Piers of Bath and Wells. In 1629
Piers tried to limit the influence of lecturers or weekday preachers
by forcing them first to read the prayers of the Church and to wear
prescribed vestments. Then in 1636 he gave orders to stop the
weekday lectures which Devenish gave on market days and went so
far as to suspend him. He also imposed a penance on Humphrey
Blake, Robert's brother and then churchwarden, for not doing his
duty by reporting Devenish for other irregularities, which included
holding Bible study sessions at his own house. But neither
Devenish nor Wootton were extreme. They may have rejoiced
when Bishop Piers and his archdeacon son were imprisoned in the
Tower as a result of complaints in the second parliament of 1640,
but they were not radicals, and in 1642 both declared for reform,
not for the removal of bishops altogether. The town was probably
with them.

St Mary's church, 1834: interior
looking east showing
Corporation pew in its original
position, in front of the chancel
screen

BUSINESS IN THE PORT

General trade improved about 1600 and receipts from customs charges
doubled. Business resumed with France, Spain and Portugal, although
direct trade was less important than coastal traffic from Bristol,
Cardiff and Barnstaple. Red, white and canary wine and sack, salt and
iron were the principal imports in the early years of the century,

Festival of Britain display in the
Blake Gardens, 1951: Mr H.E.
Bawler, Head Gardener

together with Spanish wool, raisins, sugar and sumach. Outwards went grain and other goods, largely to Ireland.

By 1615 the range of imports had narrowed a little but included exotic timber and tombstones; in the late 1630s, and probably earlier, most of the vessels in the port were plying across the Bristol Channel and coal and salt dominated business. Building materials were also of importance: cases of glass, nails and iron rods, laths and other English timber, and cotton goods called Manchester ware.

There is a tell-tale gap in the long series of accounts of the water bailiffs of the port from Michaelmas 1640 until Michaelmas 1646 which is not accidental. Individual traders were almost certainly prepared to keep in business despite the uncertainty of the times, plying in their trows, woodbushes, barques and pinnaces up and down the Bristol Channel. Coal, fish and salt were the regular commodities and in 1639–40 there was also trade in building materials, lead, iron, tallow, wool, oil; foodstuffs like currants, raisins, beef, vinegar, hops, prunes and wine; woad for dyeing, soap and even a barrel of 'painters plate'. All these goods came in more than 189 shiploads.

Six years later, when the Civil War was over, coal and salt were again the principal imports. Slightly fewer shiploads included such unlikely commodities as beer, perry, herrings, millstones, butter and sieves. During the next four years, until the accounts cease again, this time permanently, coal, salt, glass and other building materials came every year and, among the unusual items, marble, calfskins, tobacco, hardware, and more sieves and tombstones. These goods were not, of course, for Bridgwater alone. Much of the iron was sent up river to Taunton, and the coal was delivered to a wide area of Somerset and into Devon and Dorset.

THE CIVIL WAR

Men who depended on such trade were hardly in favour of its disruption, but as the country divided between king and parliament around 1640 there was little doubt where Bridgwater's sympathies lay. Until June 1643, however, it took little or no active part until half the Taunton garrison, also for parliament, retreated to Bridgwater before the royalist offensive. They did not stay long, and 2,000 men were said to have left overnight despite attempts by local folk to prevent them by manning the gates. Very soon a royalist garrison was installed, commanded by the former MP Edmund Wyndham. Prince Maurice ordered guns for his support, but he could not have felt too secure when some of his own troops mutinied after hearing a rumour that Irish soldiers had landed at Minehead or Bristol.

In the following year the situation was not much improved, for Wyndham was unable to protect some royal excise officers one market day not only from disgruntled townsmen but also from his own troops. During this time of occupation the vicar or parish clerk kept a careful record of burials of these outsiders. In the six months from June 1643 seventeen were buried. Edward Blisse was the first, killed by a sword, followed by Peter Hurman, killed by a gun. Many were described simply as 'soldier'.

In the next year there was some excitement when a troop of 500 parliamentary horse under Lt.-Gen. John Middleton attacked a royalist supply column at North Petherton. Reinforcements from the town joined Sir Francis Dodington and they managed to recover the wagons which the enemy had seized. In that year twenty-two soldiers were buried including William Kate and George Gage, 'killed at the battle of Petherton', majors Henry Killigrew and Humphrey Wharton, and Joseph Wootton, probably son or brother of George Wootton, long-time curate and soon to be vicar, killed by a cannon ball while fighting for the king at Lyme Regis. Four 'strangers' were buried at North Petherton after the fight.

Like towns throughout the country, Bridgwater found itself supporting the cause of the garrison which controlled it. The town accounts for the year from September 1644 recorded over £93 spent on 400 pairs of hose and shoes which were delivered to the king's troops at Wells. The corporation also contributed 12 gns towards guards for the town. Prince Rupert and West Country royalist leaders met in Bridgwater in April 1645, no doubt to discuss the problem of Taunton, where Edmund Wyndham had been put in charge of the royalist attempt to starve Robert Blake and the parliamentary garrison. Attention shifted back to Bridgwater in July when the royalist George Goring, driven out of Langport, brought guns and some infantry into the town.

In the early months of 1645 Bridgwater's parish register records the burials of men, often unnamed, brought back from Taunton. Among the dead were colonels Hugh Hawley, Richard Drake and Peter Mounsell, William Patten, a marshal, two standard-bearers and under-officers – a total of sixty killed by spear, sword or cannon fire, drowned or even killed in a duel. The gruesome record ends on 17 July 1645.

Four days later Gen. Massey's troops quartered at Hamp House, Col. Holbourne's at Sydenham Manor and the New Model Army

Sydenham Manor, a sixteenth-century house at the heart of an industrial complex

under Oliver Cromwell camped in the fields north of Eastover, mounted a devastating assault under the overall command of Sir Thomas Fairfax. Eastover was taken with 600 prisoners, although many of the houses had already been fired by the retreating royalists. Crossing the river with little further difficulty, Fairfax took 2,000 prisoners, 800 horse and 36 guns.

'Most of the town', so Fairfax wrote, was destroyed; less by his troops, it was later claimed, than by Col. Wyndham or the townsmen themselves. More than ten years after the siege the mayor asked for government help to repair 120 houses, including the almshouses. Many people had moved out to Wembdon to avoid the fighting.

The fall of Bridgwater was almost the end of royalist activity in Somerset, for Robert Blake's defence of Taunton had finally succeeded less than three weeks before his home town was taken. The war was virtually over, although he remained governor of Taunton and in charge of the desultory siege of Dunster until April 1646. Only then could he become politician again, for Bridgwater corporation had elected him to parliament, and he repaid their confidence by helping to persuade Fairfax to reduce the town's tax burden. His brother Humphrey, mayor in 1647, must have been among those who wanted to be rid of troops in the town, but the port provided a useful base for the expedition to Ireland. Yet people had no wish to be reminded of the devastation suffered, and some blood was spilt in 1646 when troops intervened to stop local people demolishing some of the siege works.

Crowds at the unveiling of
Blake's statue, in 1900

In that year or the next, when prospects for peace were more certain,
the corporation paid to remove guns from the quay, and in 1647–8
wine was drunk to celebrate the departure of the dragoons. More
troops were removed in the next year and normality was restored. But
that normality did not mean subservience to the new government. The
mayor chosen in 1649 was suspect and was replaced by order of the
House of Commons. The corporation returned Robert Blake to the
1654 parliament; from 1656 the other seat was taken by Sir Thomas
Wroth, still with influence and at times 'outrageously republican', but
at others a typical country gentleman.

Politics apart, what Bridgwater people needed was strong, settled
government if trade was to recover, and by 1650–1 business in the port
had at last returned to pre-war levels. But this was not the prosperity
of half a century earlier. Irish trade probably returned when the rebellion there was crushed, and there was a serious attempt to revive the
millstone business, this time with South Wales. But trade in general
was said to be stagnant, often threatened by piracy as close to home as
the Bristol Channel.

CHAPTER SIX

Dissenters and Rebels, 1660–1700

POLITICS AND PARLIAMENT

T he return of Charles II in 1660 was probably welcomed by many in the town for political reasons, but the restoration of the Church of England to its dominant place in society must have been a concern for those who for some years had enjoyed freedom to worship in one of the new traditions.

Members of the corporation were quick to change the Commonwealth crown on their maces for the royal crown and to add suitable words of loyalty. In 1661, when offering what was described as a 'voluntary gift' to the king, 136 of the most prominent men in the town and surrounding hamlets contributed, though the presence of troops may have influenced their generosity.

In the election for parliament in 1660 the corporation carefully compromised, choosing their recorder, the republican Sir Thomas Wroth, and the former royalist colonel John Tynte of Halswell. In 1661 Tynte and the former royalist commander, Edmund Wyndham, were chosen, and in the following year Tynte became the town's recorder.

When Tynte died in 1669 his seat was hotly contested by Francis Rolle of Shapwick, a nonconformist, and Peregrine Palmer, an Anglican country gentleman of Fairfield, Stogursey. Each at first received twelve votes and the mayor returned Rolle on his own casting vote, but it was soon discovered that some of Rolle's nonconformist supporters were disqualified because, against the terms of the Corporation Act which parliament had passed against nonconformists, they had permitted religious meetings – called conventicles – in their own homes. So Palmer duly took Rolle's place at Westminster.

It was a victory for the law, but nonconformists in the town grew in influence and attracted like-minded people, including several clergymen driven from their parishes in 1662 by the Act of Uniformity, which required them to accept the doctrines and practices of the Church of England. Among them, too, was John Norman, the former minister of the parish, who in 1660 left the post in favour of the former vicar, George Wootton, but had continued to serve under him with the approval of the corporation and of Wootton himself. By 1669 there were at least eleven nonconformist ministers in the town caring for eight different groups. John Norman was not then among them; he was in gaol in Ilchester for preaching without a licence.

Among the nonconformists were Presbyterians and Baptists who had been established after the Civil War and during the Commonwealth, and by 1670 a group of Quakers. Between 1660 and 1690 nonconformists were often subject to attacks for their ideas and activities. In the parish register of burials someone writing in Greek, so that few if any could understand, described faithful members of the Anglican congregation like John Roberts or John Baily as 'lover of God and of the king' or 'true lover of the king'. John Norman was generously described as a 'learned priest', and George Wootton a few months later as 'most vigilant pastor of this parish'. Under William Allen, the next vicar, there was less sympathy with nonconformists: Tobias Wells, the Baptist leader, was 'the Anabaptist holder forth'.

John Anderdon, a leading Quaker, had to endure more than Anglican insults. Although a prominent goldsmith and among the richest men in the town, he spent over twenty years in prison after his conversion, although Quakers continued to worship in his house in his absence. Some of them suffered arrest in 1670 when coming in from surrounding villages, but all were released at the request of the Anglican vicar.

There was much less sympathy shown by politicians, notably Ralph Stawell of Cothelstone, who described nonconformists as 'fanatics'. In the election of 1679 he, Sir Francis Rolle, Col. Tynte's son Halswell, and a local gentleman, William Clarke of Sandford, stood for parliament. Instead of limiting the votes to the twenty-four members of the corporation, all who paid taxes as freemen of the borough were included, an idea put forward by Stawell who arranged that members of his own regiment of militia should be able to support him. There followed a great muddle. Tynte was chosen by the members of the corporation and by the extra voters, and the fact was properly recorded in the return sealed with the borough seal. Rolle was chosen by Stawell's extra voters but the official record was only signed by the mayor and not properly sealed. Clarke came last.

Despite his efforts Stawell failed to get enough votes and was determined on revenge. In politics he was a member of the Court party, later Tory, a supporter of the king and of the Duke of York. His main opponent in the town was Sir John Malet of Enmore, who had succeeded Col. Tynte as recorder in 1669 and who was an Exclusionist, believing that the Duke of York as a Catholic should not succeed his brother. Another election in 1681 for a parliament to be held at Oxford saw Tynte returned again, this time with Malet who, his opponents declared, was now openly supported by a 'cabal of fanatics', those Whig nonconformists who feared what the duke might do if he became king. Stawell failed again.

Two years later the two parties in the town were still seriously at odds. The king's health was known to be failing and the succession of the Duke of York seemed inevitable. Scandalous political songs were being published in the town by the Whigs but, so the Tories claimed, Humphrey Steare, the mayor, would do nothing to suppress them. And he, so they claimed, dominated the town, for he was both mayor and comptroller of the port. In 1681, so another Tory claimed, Steare had forced him as a port employee to vote for Malet and not Stawell. Steare was, they said, disloyal; he had been bred in New England and had fought for Parliament during the Civil War.

Stawell's reaction was both violent and subtle. While Steare was still mayor there had been a rumour that the Presbyterian meeting house was to be attacked. Now in the summer of 1683 a detachment of militia under Stawell's command came into the town, put a guard on the homes of leading nonconformists, and set about dismantling the meeting house. It was large enough to hold 400 people, an indication of nonconformist strength, and 'made round like a cockpit' so that the pulpit stood in the centre. Anything that would burn was removed from the building and taken to the Cornhill where a bonfire 14 ft high was built, with the pulpit and its cushion on the top.

This demonstration of power at least persuaded a minority of the corporation to see things Stawell's way. During the summer he and the Bishop of Bath and Wells, the royalist Peter Mew, worked on some of the burgesses until they were prepared to hand over their charter of government to be changed, so that the Crown could have more influence, especially at elections. Stawell was in the thick of the business, naming a new recorder in place of Sir John Malet, and nominating twenty-four burgesses, 'all good men', together with two good men to serve in parliament. Stawell also suggested an 'artillery' of up to 100 men, 'loyal sons of the church' under officers chosen by himself, and the right to remove any burgess, but the government in London would not accept such extreme measures.

But the next election, on the death of Charles II, did not produce the result Stawell and the government wanted. The new recorder, Sir Francis Warre, was returned safely enough, but Stawell's other candidate, a major in his regiment of militia, was beaten by the local influence of Sir Halswell Tynte, despite the machinations of the new mayor, who described his opponents on the corporation as 'grindallizing self-willed humourists', and so rotten he had to open their post.

MONMOUTH'S REBELLION AND THE BATTLE OF SEDGEMOOR

Only half a victory at the election was followed by the choice of a Whig mayor, Alexander Popham, who was supported by a majority of Whigs on the corporation. They were a sympathetic enough group to greet the arrival of the Duke of Monmouth and some 4,000 armed men after his proclamation as king in Taunton. Stawell's militia went over to the rebels in their hundreds. Monmouth, the hope of the Whigs and nonconformists, had raised much of East Devon, Dorset and South Somerset; and among his trusted lieutenants, in charge of Taunton's Blue regiment, was Col. Richard Bovett, well known in Bridgwater for his activities as the rule of the Commonwealth came to an end. John Boone, the town's watchman, was paid handsomely for 'being upon duty night and day when Monmouth was coming'.

So on 21 June 1685 the corporation of Bridgwater, unlike their fellows in Taunton, had no hesitation. The mayor and burgesses 'in their formalities' proclaimed Monmouth king and the town did more than any other to support the cause, offering Castle Field for a camp, giving the duke quarters in the castle, and raising money by voluntary contributions. Two men were later given particular credit, Roger Hoar and William Coleman, the one a prosperous mercer and leading member of the Presbyterian meeting, the other a farmer.

The rebels stayed overnight and then left for Glastonbury, their ranks swelled now by 500 men with their 'cruel and murthering' scythes. How many townsmen actually joined is something of a puzzle. A smaller and less cheerful army returned on 4 July, but the town now had a special part to play. The rebel paymaster had summoned carpenters and labourers there with their tools, spades and wheelbarrows, but perhaps only to suggest that they would stand and fight the royal army which was not far behind. The town's defences were certainly much weaker than they had been in 1645 – a small cannon in the castle, two at the High Cross, one at the south gate, and a barricade at the bridge. More likely a breakout of cavalry was planned, for at Sandford the rebels relieved Mr Clarke of food, saddles and bridles, and tried unsuccessfully to 'borrow' a large sum in cash.

But whatever the plan, it was changed when Richard Godfrey came into town from Chedzoy to describe to Monmouth how the royal army was camped on the moor. From St Mary's tower he confirmed the unlikely tale that the king's troops were rather casually deployed on the Weston side of the Bussex Rhyne and might be surprised by a frontal attack, just the sort of bold move Monmouth had learnt from his years of fighting on the continent.

How some 4,000 men including 600 horse could have left the town at dead of night under the noses of royalist spies is either miracle or mystery. Most of them had been camped beyond the river and could have moved across fields without too much noise. Led by the Red regiment a silent column marched up the Bristol road and turned down Bradney Lane, along Marsh Lane and around Peasy Farm, avoiding the prying eyes of Parson Paschall of Chedzoy and his parishioners. Beyond the farm the foot halted to let the horse go by, and they all disappeared into the mist. Most of the rebels who fought in the battle that followed were scattered across the moor before the devastating fire of the royal guns, themselves eventually trained in the right direction through the help of an unlikely 'officer', none other than Bishop Peter Mew, by now promoted to be Bishop of Winchester but still no friend of the Bridgwater Whigs. Some 150 men of the Red regiment retired in reasonable order back to the town, and a few escaped including their commanding officer, Nathaniel Wade, who reached North Devon before his arrest. The pursuing royal forces took longer to get to the town, their attention concentrated on rounding up and hanging stragglers. While the morning of 6 July was still quite young, John, Lord Churchill (later Duke of Marlborough) and Col. Kirke occupied Bridgwater with the Foot Guards and troops of cavalry.

But victory has its cost, just like defeat. One estimate put rebel losses at 700 dead and about 300 taken. The royal army lost 27 dead and 200 wounded, and those wounded had to be cared for; 110 were brought to the town, and their care was perhaps not best guaranteed if local surgeons bore serious personal grudges.

Perhaps that is why so few locals appeared at the assizes before Jefferies and his fellow judges. Just seventeen men from Bridgwater including, of course, Roger Hoar and William Coleman, and eight men from Durleigh were among the thirty or so rebels held in Bridgwater prison or elsewhere in the county. Roger Hoar may, indeed, have been regarded in some sense as the town's guarantee of good behaviour. He was presumably held in gaol in Wells until the assizes there in late September, when he was sentenced to be hanged in his home town. A dramatic last-minute reprieve still left him in custody until February 1686 when a pardon was granted under the Great Seal, no doubt at a considerable price.

It is curious that so little survives of these dramatic events among Bridgwater's records: just a payment to the executioner of a shilling by the town's receiver 'for takinge the Ropes of the Galows', the man's official reward for his gruesome services after nine rebels had been hanged, drawn and quartered in the town, including men from Huntspill and North Petherton. However, the government's Treasury Books record that £19 16*s* was paid out by the Physician-General to the Forces 'for the pay of chirurgeons [surgeons] hired to dress the wounded soldiers'; and also that, two years after the battle, the mayor and corporation were given £60 'for meat, drink and other necessaries by them furnished to the sick and wounded soldiers there'.

A year after the rebellion King James himself came westwards and on 27 August 1686 arrived in Bridgwater with his formidable retinue late in the afternoon after preparations costing the town a mere 2*s*. He rode with some suspicion across Sedgemoor from Chedzoy to Weston, and went back to the town for the night. The next day he returned to the safer surroundings of Wells; Taunton he avoided.

Neither king nor government felt secure after such a serious rebellion, and Bridgwater had to suffer the presence of dragoons in the town, quartered at local expense, for at least a year. In 1687 the Declaration of Indulgence permitting freedom of worship for nonconformists was not greeted with great enthusiasm, for the corporation had changed its political complexion and was now Tory in sympathy. But, in a reversal of the policy of 1683, seven of the leading Tories were now removed. In 1689 the town elected two Tories to the parliament which offered the throne to William of Orange, and effectively established the liberty for which Monmouth and the Whigs had fought.

The Whigs were still not in total control of the corporation but managed to elect Roger Hoar to parliament in 1695 and 1698. He died in 1699, a leading Presbyterian, owner of the manor of Hamp, which he had bought from Bristol corporation the year before, and representative of a huge number of nonconformists who included about six hundred Presbyterians, about 200 Baptists, and a body of Quakers who had built a new meeting house for another 200 people. The town, if not yet the corporation, was Whig; in favour of religious toleration and enterprise, against government interference.

CHAPTER SEVEN

Enterprise and Corruption, 1700–1835

THE CORPORATION AND POLITICS

Toleration by the law did not mean toleration of each other, and for much of the eighteenth century members of the corporation were divided among themselves; old scores were not yet settled.

The formal records of the corporation's regular business survive today only from 1717, almost certainly because of legal actions where earlier records were used as evidence and not returned. One case was brought in 1717–18 by Roger Hoar the younger, James Bowles and Robert Methwen against the mayor, Nicholas Jeffreys, Ferdinando Anderdon and others. Methwen called the mayor 'an inconsiderate puppy, rascal, blockhead, numskull'; Hoar and others were accused of disloyalty to the Crown in failing to join in prayers for the king (Hoar declared he always knelt in church except when he had gout); Anderdon was declared to have spoken in favour of the Pretender. Arguments involved claims that the 1683 charter was not legal and that a majority of the corporation would not accept the loyalty of nonconformists who had taken the oath of occasional conformity. Hoar, Methwen and other nonconformists thus refused to attend meetings to prevent business being transacted. The rest removed them from office but were forced to accept them back.

Despite such unseemly squabbling, the dignity of the town's governors had to be preserved. In 1725 vicar Lawrence Paine began a morning service before the mayor and corporation had taken their seats, and they not only complained about him to the archdeacon but tried to reduce his salary. In 1728 one member brought an action against the mayor for 'slyly and clandestinely' organizing the appointment of a new colleague. In 1730 John Webber had to be removed as town clerk on account of age, abuses and mistakes; in 1733 the recorder was asked to remove his deputy who had abused the mayor; in 1737 the receiver admitted 'many discrepancies' in the town accounts.

Peace then seems to have reigned until the 1770s, although in 1768 one of the aldermen attacked the mayor for illegally increasing the number of voters at a parliamentary election. There were disputed elections to the corporation in 1771, 1774 and 1784, the last involving a court hearing in London and the claim that since one man had been unlawfully chosen three years earlier, all council business during that time had also been illegal. The dispute lasted several months and involved the dismissal of the recorder, Vere Poulett, in favour of the politician Charles James Fox. Poulett was reinstated because the corporation found they could not afford to oppose his claim for unfair dismissal. The year 1798 saw another dispute when the retiring mayor walked out with some of his friends, leaving no quorum to choose his successor.

The Poulett-Fox rivalry was part of wider national politics. For more than half a century George Bubb Dodington, Lord Melcombe, and his father had nominated one of the town's MPs in the Whig interest, and the corporation had allowed a Tory country gentleman to take the other. After 1753 the Pouletts of Hinton St George had most influence, but the Percevals of Enmore attempted to gain power, and in the 1780s one group of Whigs in the town favoured Fox and the others Lord North. After the turn of the century both members were Tories for some time. A Whig and a Tory represented the town when the Reform Bill became law.

In all this the corporation seems to have shown little independence of action, and it can hardly be claimed that they were assiduous in their obligations as rectors responsible for the fabric of the parish church. In 1724, when repairs were needed to the roof, they found materials cheaply by demolishing part of the ancient St Mary's cross. In 1738 they saved on the cost of new galleries by using the old ones no longer needed in the assize hall. But in 1743 they were happy to repair their own pew and provided twenty-four 'handsome folio Common Prayer Books with the Town Arms'. In 1775 the large painting Anne Poulett had given to the corporation was found a home above the altar.

The seal of the corporation in use in the eighteenth century, depicting a castle on a bridge over a river

TRADE

At the end of the seventeenth century Bridgwater merchants could reasonably claim naval protection: Roger Hoar the elder and his partners in the 1690s lost four ships in the Bristol Channel in eighteen months, one taken out of Milford Haven by a French privateer. The war with France certainly changed the direction of trade, and West Country ports began to bring in Irish wool for local clothiers. Among the people taking advantage of the change was William Alloway, who traded out of Minehead, Watchet and Bridgwater and whose main business up to 1704 was in wool and tallow from Dublin, Cork and Waterford, but who imported rock salt from Liverpool, tobacco from Antigua, and coal, white soap and fish. Among the business recorded in one of his surviving ledgers was a cargo of 515 barrels of white herrings and 98 barrels of red herrings taken on the *Unity* to Barbados.

Coastal trade was more important to Bridgwater in the eighteenth century than foreign business, and the peak was probably reached in the 1750s and 1760s. By that time coal, culm, deals, small masts and pipestaves were classed as the main foreign imports, while coastal imports comprised beer, cider, glass bottles, beef, bricks, cheese, bacon and wood hoops. Outward trade was largely in corn to Bristol. These were official statistics, and they were accompanied by statements that during the period 1758–63 there had been no foreign vessels in the port and that smuggling was not allowed. Certainly,

The second Town Bridge, cast at Coalbrookdale in 1795 and finished in 1798

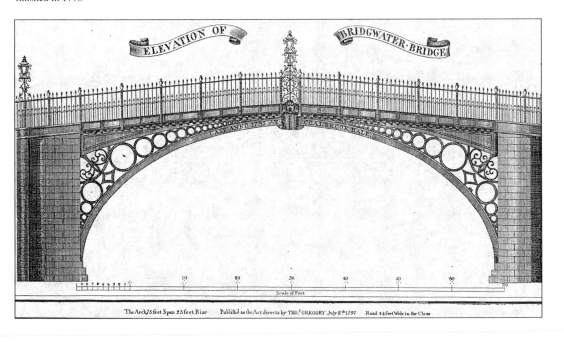

Bridgwater's corn exports had been remarked upon in the 1720s, when wheat and local cloth called Bridgwater plains (half red, half deep blue) had been shipped from Bristol to Madeira; and the *Mercury*, coming from Gallipoli and Leghorn, had been found to contain illegal rum. Risks of wartime trading were shown by the experience of the *Diana* of Bridgwater, owned by local merchant Philip Baker, who in 1740 was permitted to operate as a privateer. Five years later the ship was taken on its way to its wartime base in Newfoundland.

The import of bricks may at first seem curious and is presumably explained because the local demand was greater than supply. Among those buying local bricks from the 1760s was Thomas Kymer, who used them in his coal mines near Kidwelly, and in return produced culm and anthracite dust used for burning in Bridgwater kilns.

By the end of the eighteenth century thirty-two vessels belonged to the port, and trade was mostly in coal and timber. There was also some trade with Portugal and Newfoundland, and twenty years earlier there had been contacts with the Gibraltar Straits and Virginia. Trade in Irish wool remained significant.

THE BEGINNINGS OF INDUSTRY

The enterprise of William Alloway and his trading successors was for a short time also found within the town. Presumably in the hope of creating a political base James Brydges, the wealthy Duke of Chandos, bought the castle and adjoining properties in 1721 and proposed to build houses on the site. At about the same time he invested large sums of money to make soap, cloth, rope and glass bottles, build ships and establish a distillery. Some of the houses were finished at enormous cost, but all the industrial enterprises had collapsed within fifteen years, and only the bottle kiln survived.

Shipbuilding under other management was much more successful. About 1697 John Trott built the *Friendship* for William Alloway, and he or his son of the same name in 1729, working on the east bank of the river near the present bus station, continued the business. A year earlier the remarkable Dr John Allen, physician and inventor, had written a treatise about making docks, and in 1732 a committee of the corporation began to negotiate with perhaps a third John Trott (he was only twenty-four years old) about building one where his father had been removing clay to make bricks. The dock was ready in 1736 and Trott himself leased it from the corporation. Seven years later he agreed to install gates to make it a dry dock. Yet another John Trott was still operating the dock in 1814. Here, presumably, repairs were

Experiment in concrete: Castle House, Queen Street

carried out on many ships; elsewhere on the river banks some forty new ships were built during the period 1766–99.

The other successful enterprise firmly established in the eighteenth century was brickmaking. In the 1680s George Balch and Thomas Christopher made enough to rebuild the dam across the Durleigh brook by the Town mill and to rebuild or repair the Cockmoyle prison. By 1709 a brick kiln was working at Hamp; and Hugh Tilsley, brick and pantile maker, was admitted a freeman of the borough in 1738. Edmund Sealy was in business with his father at Hamp by 1776. By 1810 he owned several ships and employed 'a whole colony' of people on his brick grounds. A dozen years later there were three firms of brickmakers at Hamp and another with offices in King Square, and by 1830 there were five, including the Sealy family, John Browne and William Dudderidge Champion, the last of whom in 1827 had taken out a patent for ornamental bricks. Bridgwater's main industry was firmly established.

A TOUCH OF ELEGANCE

Elegance arrived in Bridgwater towards the end of the seventeenth-century when the Harvey family, owners of the castle, created a water garden and planted a large grove of elm trees. In 1690–1 the corporation commissioned a copper weather vane to crown their pavilion at the bowling green across the river, and not many years later a coffee house was opened just off Fore Street. Such signs of finesse were given a focus from 1720, when the town secured regular visits each August by the assize judges.

Thus was created a short season when the town was thronged with county society. The temporary 'boarder house' provided in 1720 for the courts was quickly replaced by an assize hall built in High Street, on the site of the Red Cow inn. The building would guarantee that the judges would continue to come to the town, so members of the corporation actually put up the cost themselves and then proceeded to recoup from a levy on the town's innkeepers. Members of the corporation and innkeepers would benefit equally.

The season included plays at the town hall and dancing at the guildhall, although vandalism ended the dancing for a time. Miss Feilding and her company of Bath Comedians came outside the season in 1736 and played for six weeks in the unoccupied assize hall, where they had to build their own stage and provide seats. In 1755 it was decided to lay a new deal floor in the guildhall 'for the ensuing horse race', presumably for the balls which were an essential part of

Barham's Brickworks, East Quay

High Street, *c.* 1800, from an etching by J. Chubb. The buildings in the centre of the street, on the site of the medieval shambles, include the colonnaded Assize Hall

society diversions. Horse races became a regular feature, attracting subscriptions from politicians such as Charles James Fox, and in 1813 Taunton Races transferred to the town – or rather to Chilton Common. By the 1820s, if not earlier, they were held in September rather than August, but popular amusements took their place – public breakfasts, balls and backsword play were advertised 'as usual' on the common in 1793, and in the town the theatrical folk came, by 1813 attracting Henry Lee and his company with the possibilities of good audiences. Edmund Keane appeared in the 1816 season. Two years earlier enthusiasm for peace had produced a feast for up to 1,000 people on the Cornhill; diners at twenty massive trestle tables had only to bring their own knives, forks and chairs.

Another kind of elegance appeared in the new houses in Castle and Chandos streets although those were not the earliest brick buildings in the town; one with a 'cupillo or tower' was certainly earlier. The original Chandos plan was for a wide street, each side with six houses of five bays, all of three storeys in brick with ashlar string courses and bolection-moulded architraves. They were probably designed by Benjamin Holloway. Holloway's own fine house, The Lions, was built a

Poster for Bridgwater Races, 1794

Bridgwater Amufements, 1794.

ON THURSDAY the Twenty-firft of AUGUST next
will be run for on Chilton Common, near Bridgwater, by any Horfe, Mare, or
Gelding, that never won the value of TWENTY POUNDS, at any one time, (matches
excepted) and being (bona fide) the Property of Gentlemen refident in the County of Somerfet, and that have been ufed as HUNTERS, or on the ROAD, this laft
Seafon, (of which proper Certificates muft be produced), carrying twelve Stone,
the beft of three four mile Heats,

A LARGE HANDSOME
SILVER CUP,

of the real value of TWENTY POUNDS, given by the Gentlemen of the
Town and Neighbourhood of BRIDGWATER.

Alfo, a Saddle & Bridle

will be run for between the heats by Ponies that never won any thing.

AND on FRIDAY the Twenty-fecond of Auguft next
will be run for at the fame place, by any Horfe, Mare, or Gelding, that never
won FIFTY POUNDS at any one time, weight for age, according to New Market
Cup weights, the beft of three four mile Heats.

A LARGE HANDSOME
SILVER CUP,

of the real value of TWENTY POUNDS, given by the Gentlemen of the
Town and Neighbourhood of TAUNTON.

Alfo, a Saddle and Bridle

will be run for between the Heats, by Hacks that never won any thing.
Each Horfe &c. to pay Half-a-guinea Entrance, or double at the Poft.
A clear Heat each day for the Stakes. Not lefs than three to ftart each Day.
Difputes to be determined by a majority of fubfcribers of One Guinea.
To Start each Day at four in the Afternoon.
The winer (each day) to pay Five-fhillings for Weights and Scales.
The Horfes to be fhown and entered at the Crown Inn in Bridgwater, on Wednef-
day the 20th of Auguft next, between the hours of four and feven in the After-

The elegance of Castle Street
(1724–34) and King Square
(*c.* 1820) from the river

little later on West Quay. Other elegant buildings still surviving from
the century are Waterloo House and the original part of The Priory in
Mary Street and No. 5 West Quay. They are in an English baroque
style which was followed later in the century by a more restrained
design typified by King Square and some of the houses in High Street,
where the medieval shambles were removed in the early 1820s.
Among the new buildings are the Town Hall (1823) and, in the
Cornhill, the pillared market house of about 1827.

These new buildings required better surroundings. In 1724 the Duke
of Chandos was allowed by the corporation to make a drain to carry
away water from his proposed new street. Twenty years later a man
was permitted to put up a fence in front of his house to protect his
glass windows from passers-by – presumably because of increased
traffic. Improving the main streets came within the province of the

The Cornhill and St Mary's church, 1832. The Market House now graces the centre of the town and the streets have been widened

turnpike trustees from 1730, but not until 1778 did a general town meeting put pressure on the corporation to improve the very narrow St Mary Street and its cramped approach to the Cornhill. An Act of Parliament of 1779 enabled money to be raised to pave, light and watch the town's streets and footpaths as well as to regulate the markets. A second act, repeating much of the first, suggests that little was done.

But that was perhaps to be expected, for the corporation did not see itself as existing for the benefit of the town unless that benefit might also accrue to its own members. The Revd Richard Jenkins Runwa Jenkins served as mayor several times. He was, wrote a fellow clergyman, 'vain, insolent and ostentatious' but still a good mayor, for in the difficult times of the spring of 1800 he bought up a cargo of potatoes to sell to the poor. Charity was one thing; the modern notion of public service another.

The Cornhill in 1953:
pedestrians and traffic kept
apart

CHAPTER EIGHT

Reform and Renewal, 1835–1914

A NEW BEGINNING

I n 1833 someone described the corporation as 'self elected, and irresponsible and . . . now so admirably constituted that five of its members with their sons and grandsons can always command a majority'. Only a year or two earlier the bishop had instructed two members, both Anglican clergymen, to resign their places, since it was obviously no fit position for them to hold. National moves towards a more representative style of local government brought commissioners enquiring into the town's affairs. They found the corporation deep in debt as the result of the private bankruptcy of the borough treasurer; they agreed that members did not 'fairly' represent the inhabitants and had been in the habit of interfering with parliamentary elections. They also found that expenditure in 1835, £945, was greater than income at £936.

After the passing of the Municipal Corporations Act the old corporation, set up in 1468 and operating under the charter of 1683, was dissolved. In its place, just after Christmas 1835, the ratepayers of the borough elected eighteen councillors, eight from the south ward, nine from the north, with a chairman. Three days later six of those were chosen aldermen, and on 1 January 1836 Thomas Withy Inman became the first mayor under the new constitution. The change was revolutionary. Only one of the new council, Frederick Axford, had belonged to the old corporation; the new men were more closely bound up with the commercial life of the town. Of the six men chosen at the next election, one was a merchant, one a tanner, one a pawnbroker and one an innkeeper.

The new town government meant business: they created committees for the watch, finance, the port and navigation, and later property and

The improved town, *c*. 1840. The new Royal Clarence Hotel, opened in 1825, signals the beginning of the rebuilt High Street

tithe matters, and by March 1837 had drawn up very modest estimates. Road repairs were put at £200, salaries of clergy and officers at £150 15*s*, police £55, charities £50, cost of keeping prisoners £50, public buildings £50 and sundries £100.

Gradually, as the century progressed, the corporation became concerned with matters of wider public concern. From 1845 they took over full responsibility for the Parrett navigation; in 1857 they succeeded the old market trustees and thereafter controlled the market and paved and lit the streets; from 1867 they became concerned with public health, from 1876 with water supply, from 1877 with free libraries. By the 1890s there were committees for allotments and town improvements; from 1904 they became an education authority.

Thus water, since 1694 drawn from the Durleigh brook along wooden pipes to the cistern over the High Cross, from 1875 came from Ashford reservoir via Wembdon Hill. Gas was made in Taunton Road from 1834, and electricity was introduced in 1904. Other public services improved by the new corporation included the borough police, formed in 1835 with headquarters first in Fore Street by the old gaol, later in High Street, and from 1911 in Northgate. The fire service was still a matter for the churchwardens of St Mary's in the 1830s, when the fire engine was kept by the poorhouse near the south gate. By the 1880s it was housed by the corporation behind the Town Hall, where the fire station remained until 1964.

The seal of the corporation on the gates of Blake Gardens

BRIBERY AND CORRUPTION

The reforms effected by the Municipal Corporations Act had both good and bad consequences. There was evidently more responsible government, but party politics began, neither for the first nor for the last time, to play a role in local government. The triumphant Whigs on taking power in Bridgwater immediately began to apply the principle of political appointments by relieving John Trevor, the town clerk, of his influential post. From that time onwards even the most insignificant office holder was subject to political scrutiny. In these circumstances it is hardly surprising that parliamentary elections should have become occasions for acute party rivalry; but in Bridgwater they also became the opportunity for bribery and corruption on a scale more common a century earlier.

There were 568 voters registered for the election held in May 1837 when one of the sitting Whig members, John Temple Leader, accepted the Chiltern Hundreds in order to contest a vacant seat in the City of Westminster. The Tory Henry Broadwood and the Whig Richard Brinsley Sheridan, both outsiders, stood for the vacant seat, and Broadwood was returned by 279 votes to 221, thanks to bribes given to at least 153 voters. The facts were so well known that Broadwood nearly resigned on the threat of a petition to Parliament against him, but he was saved by the death of the king and the consequent dissolution of Parliament.

The story of the election was, however, unfolded in a case brought by a man called Webb, an informer, against Richard Smith, a Bridgwater pawnbroker and the Tories' bribery agent. During that trial, held at Taunton in the spring of 1838, Lord Chief Justice Denman and a special jury heard about a 'low fellow' from London, one Croucher, who hired himself from borough to borough as 'The Man in the Moon' to organize bribery for either party. His exploits at Bridgwater had evidently been entirely successful.

The first election of Queen Victoria's reign, in July 1837, was another Tory triumph. Broadmead stood again, this time with Philip Courtenay, a 'wealthy stranger', whose ability to finance success was well established. Both sides, for the first time, brought in national party managers, the Tory MP William Holmes and the Whig Mr Coppock. The two Whigs, Sir Thomas Lethbridge from Sandhill, well known in the town, and Richard Sheridan, were led to believe (by people bribed to pretend they were Whig supporters) that success was assured without the need for spending money. The result was that they received seven votes between them. Sheridan, grandson of the playwright, soon found a parliamentary home at Shaftesbury. A petition against the Bridgwater result met with little support and no enquiry was made. There were attractions in being a Bridgwater voter.

Votes were worth between £40 and £50 at the 1841 election when Broadwood was joined on the Tory side by Thomas Seaton Forman, a Welsh iron merchant. Edward Drew from Devon and Augustine Robinson, a very rich barrister, acquitted themselves reasonably well for the Whigs, but still failed to win either seat.

By 1847, the year of the next election, local attorneys had gained control of political affairs. John Trevor, the former town clerk, managed matters for the Tories, Benjamin Lovibond, aided by Thomas Ford, the new town clerk, worked for the Whigs. Until almost the last minute there were only two candidates, Colonel C.K. Kemeys Tynte of Halswell for the Whigs and Broadwood again for the Tories. Tynte had evidently done a deal with some of the Tories, and there were those who believed that Mr Sergeant Gazelee was introduced as a third candidate simply to encourage bribery. He himself, standing as a 'Purity' candidate, could hardly have seen it that way; his total expenses were £26. Tynte received 395 votes, Broadwood 265 and Gazelee 196.

Five years later and the Whigs were still split, the 'Tyntites' continuing their agreement with the opposition to ensure that the Colonel was returned. So there were five candidates, Brent Spenser Follett of the Chancery Bar and J.C. Mansell, who were supported by the Tory attorneys; the local writer A.W. Kinglake and Lord Henley for the Liberals, the latter attempting to 'open' the borough and free it from the Liberal attorneys; and Colonel Tynte, supported by both parties. In the event Tynte received 272 votes, Follett 244, Mansell 177, Lord Henley 149 and Kinglake only 101. Bribery was only slight but argument was fierce; the conflict was 'more acrid' in the borough than in the country at large.

The Liberals patched up their differences on the eve of the 1857 election, caused by a ministerial crisis, and Tynte and Kinglake won handsomely against only one Tory, although it was clear that Kinglake had been chosen because he was less averse to financial transactions than the 'pure' Lord Henley. Fifteen people are known to have given bribes and eleven to have received them, but no petition against the result was presented.

Two years later Tynte and Kinglake stood against two wealthy Tory 'strangers', Henry Padwick and Henry Westropp. Cash flowed openly, the Tyntes paying their supporters with £10 notes and Padwick giving his agent at least £2,000 for distribution. It was later reckoned that 140 voters accepted bribes. Tynte and Kinglake were again returned, and this time a petition against the result was presented, only to be with-drawn on the promise that a libel case against the *Bridgwater Times* would be dropped.

Between 1865 and 1868 Bridgwater voters enjoyed four elections. Westropp topped the poll in July 1865 with 328 votes; second came Kinglake with 257. Kinglake and his unsuccessful fellow Liberal, Sir John Shelley, then petitioned against Westropp, and the Select Committee of the House of Commons, at last dealing with Bridgwater's disease, found that 173 voters, more than a quarter of the electorate, had been bribed and that twenty-five of Westropp's sup-porters were guilty of bribery or corrupt practices. Westropp was duly unseated.

Exactly what these corrupt practices were may be read in the pub-lished minutes of evidence heard by the Select Committee and later published by Parliament. Witnesses, at least one very unwell, were summoned to London, and between 17 and 25 April 1866 members of the committee or their counsel asked 6,525 questions. One of the first witnesses was John Cooze, keeper of the North Pole beerhouse, who said he had been approached by Thomas Boys, clerk in the office of Smith and Sons, Bridgwater solicitors. 'If so be you can get some money out of the low party,' Boys declared, 'I will give you £30 and that money back again.' Further questions elicited the fact that the low party, whose colours were purple and orange, were the Liberals. Cooze evidently assented to the arrangement and was taken to the Bull and Butcher for free beer and on to the Albion where he was given two 'cartridges' of blue paper. Much to the annoyance of Boys he checked that the contents of the 'cartridges' were not farthings but ten sovereigns before giving both his votes (a plumper) to Westropp as Boyes stood behind him.

John Staples, a master mariner and part owner of a vessel in the port, told a similar story. He had been approached in Fore Street by a man with 'a speckly-coloured hat, and blue ribbons, and rather pock-marked', whose identity was established as Edward Stroud, formerly a Bridgwater druggist but at the time a publican in Burnham. Staples was instructed to follow Stroud to the water closet in the market where the promise was given to support Westropp. Both then adjourned to the Clarence.

The same kind of story was repeated many times during those few days, the last being the evidence of Benjamin Lovibond, the ailing election agent of Sir John Shelley for this election, and for many years before that agent for Colonel Tynte. He proved to be a most difficult witness, managing to avoid incriminating questions and categorically denying the claims of one Hayward, a hairdresser, whose attitude must have been common among voters: an election was an opportunity to make money. Lovibond claimed that Hayward had asked him for money in return for his vote. Lovibond insisted he had met Hayward but once and then as a customer. Hayward claimed he had been offered a bribe. The sum of £50 was mentioned because, so he claimed to have told Lovibond, he was 'oddly circumstanced at present, you know; I have laid out a great deal of money in altering my rooms; and, in addition to that, I have erected a new machine for brushing hair; I have done it on borrowed money, and I owe £50 which I must clear off at this election, and intend to'.

The conclusion of the Select Committee was inevitable, but Kinglake's return was allowed to stand, and he was later to claim that he knew of no such practices on his behalf. The Committee, ever cautious, thought there 'was reason to believe that corrupt practices' had become 'extremely prevalent'.

A by-election to replace the unseated Westropp in June 1866 returned George Patton with a majority of only seven over the economist Walter Bagehot from Langport. Within a month Patton was appointed Lord Advocate for Scotland and had therefore to face the electorate again. This time he lost to Philip Vanderbyl. In the first by-election it was later proved that 231 voters had received bribes, in the second 290 voters.

These figures were discovered during enquiries made after the election of November 1868. Bribery this time was on a much smaller scale, partly because the electorate had now increased to as many as 1,500. The voters placed Kinglake at the top of the poll with 731, followed closely by Vanderbyl with 725, Henry Westropp with 681 and Charles William Gray with 650: another Liberal victory, but short-lived. The defeated Tories petitioned against the result and their case was heard in Bridgwater Town Hall before Mr Justice Blackburn in February 1869. He reported to the Commons Select Committee that the victors were guilty of bribery and recommended that a commission should be set up to enquire into the behaviour of the Bridgwater electors over the past thirty years.

Between August and October 1869 the commission sat for forty-seven days, examined 515 people and asked a total of 47,548 questions. Their conclusion was devastating but just. Bridgwater Borough could no longer be a separate constituency; bribery and corruption had to be put down. The town lost a right which had no place in a changing world.

THE GROWTH OF THE TOWN

Between 1801, the year of the first official census, and 1911, Bridgwater's population increased nearly five times, from 3,634 to 17,981; increases were especially rapid between 1801 and 1841 and in the first ten years of the twentieth century. The increases were partly due to improved health standards, although the cholera epidemic of 1849 caused a great scare; and partly because new and expanding business such as engineering and brick and tile making offered employment. The increases brought with them problems of poverty associated with seasonal trade, and inevitable overcrowding.

New streets of houses began to be built, first south and later east of the town, and the Church of England responded by building two new churches and creating new parishes around them carved out of the old parish of St Mary's. Holy Trinity church, Taunton Road, was consecrated in 1840 and St John the Baptist's church, Eastover, in 1846, the latter one of the first in the country to embody the principles of the Oxford Movement. Among the first new streets in Holy Trinity parish were Albert and Victoria streets, and in St John's parish were Church

Holy Trinity church. Wash drawing by J.C. Buckler, 1840

Holy Trinity interior,
photographed *c*. 1890

Street, Blake Place, and the terraces in Monmouth Street and along the
Bristol and Bath roads.

The arrival of the railway on the east side of the town gave further
impetus to expansion. By 1861 St John Street, leading to the station,
had become a shopping centre and from that date there was almost
continuous building: Devonshire Street, Edward Street, Rosebery
Avenue and, in 1905–6, Cranleigh Gardens. A new church on the eastern edge of town, All Saints, opened in 1882. By the 1880s houses
were being built in St Saviour's Avenue (named after a medieval
chapel outside the town's south gate) and Taunton Road. Westwards
the town expanded into Wembdon and Durleigh parishes, beginning in
the terraces of Provident Place in the 1850s where an early type of
building society provided model houses for labourers, mostly in the
brick and tile industry. The centre of the town was also being
improved, but there still remained cramped courts off Friarn Street,
north of High Street, and around West Street, which were not removed
until the next century.

Mid-Victorian town houses,
Monmouth Street

The YMCA building, erected 1887, Salmon Parade and Eastover

RELIGION AND RECREATION

In 1826 the corporation agreed to pay for a decorated plaster ceiling in the chancel of St Mary's church but were apparently reluctant to repair crumbling battlements, despite receiving a substantial income from the tithes of the parish. In 1815 the vicar, William Wollen, who had held office since 1786, had reported to the bishop that he held two services every Sunday and read prayers on Wednesdays, Fridays and festivals, but that he had no vicarage house fit to live in. He was also incumbent of Chilton. In 1825 the bishop wrote to the corporation urging them to pay for an extra Sunday service, but the corporation refused. By 1827 the vicar was assisted by his son James, and by 1835 he was also serving as rector of Kilton. Mr Wollen remained vicar until 1844, evidently quite unmoved by the changes taking place in other parts of the Church of England, although the two new churches in the town were soon to put the old parish church to shame.

Action had to be taken because long neglect of St Mary's had made it unsafe, but the young architect appointed to save the church,

West Street on St Matthew's
Fair Day, 1907

W.H. Brakspear, changed it almost beyond recognition between 1849
and 1853, much to the dismay of many national experts. Only a short-
age of money and doubts about the foundations prevented him from
tearing down the spire and tower and replacing it with something
much taller and quite out of character with the local style. In the event
he was allowed to recreate something of the medieval splendour in a
flamboyant Gothic of his own design, incorporating a few fragments
of original woodwork, much to the confusion of visitors.

The new building, the pride of the town, came alive under the
leadership of William Wollen's successors. A surpliced choir was
introduced in 1849, beginning the church's long and distinguished
musical tradition, and its spiritual life revived under the Tractarian
Michael Sadler, vicar from 1857 to 1864. By 1870 there were three
services each Sunday and several during the week, and celebrations of
Holy Communion twice a month.

Revival also took place among the nonconformists in the town,
where the older denominations were joined by the Mariners Christian
church in 1837, the Plymouth Brethren and the Catholic Apostolic
church by 1840, three new branches of Methodism in the 1850s and
1860s and the Salvation Army in 1880. These and the other nonconformist churches established day and Sunday schools which offered
education to the growing number of children in the town.

Education could also be found in the reading rooms opened from
the 1830s and in the museum founded in 1861. The magistrates evidently did not find the theatre suitable and withdrew its licence in
1853, but other entertainment could be found in watching or playing
cricket from 1832, attending the horse races again from 1854, going to

St Mary's church from the
south-east, showing pierced
parapet and gable and
fourteenth-century style tracery

81

Bridgwater Carnival, 1933: members of the North Pole Inn Carnival Club have become the Norfolk and Suffolk Borderers of 1831

the three annual fairs, from 1890 swimming in the baths in Old Taunton Road or, from the beginning of the twentieth century, strolling in the Blake Gardens or Eastover recreation ground or visiting the Bijou Theatre.

Special to Bridgwater was the annual bonfire on the Cornhill to commemorate the Gunpowder Plot. In the 1850s the event took on political overtones, and in 1857 the crushing of the Indian Mutiny inspired a procession, the first to be called a carnival, involving decorated floats, a band, and firework displays called 'squibbing'. There were spectacular processions in 1882 and 1883, the second celebrating the completion of the new bridge over the Parrett. In 1884 there was a more organized carnival, the first in a long line which has made the town famous. The last bonfire was held on the Cornhill in 1924.

INDUSTRY AND COMMERCE

Bridgwater became Somerset's leading industrial town in the nineteenth century, its prosperity based on engineering, shipbuilding and the manufacture of bricks and tiles. The firms of John Sealy, Henry James Major, and John Browne and Co. were the most prominent of the makers of bricks and tiles, the whole industry in the 1840s employing about 1,300 people. About 1850 there were sixteen yards within two miles of the town bridge on both banks of the Parrett, and according to the 1851 census there were living in Bridgwater parish

Workers at John Board's
brickyard, *c.* 1910

thirty-seven brickmakers, seventeen tilemakers, ninety-six brickmaker's labourers, 104 brickyard labourers, three burners, one carter and three foremen. Among the skilled bricklayers working in and around the town was one employing six men and six boys.

By 1881 there were fifty-seven tilemakers, twenty-nine skilled brickmakers and nearly 250 labourers out of a total of 355 in the trade. Others lived in neighbouring parishes, for H.J. Major then employed 120 men and 100 boys. Barhams, a much more modest business, employed eighteen men and four boys; one yard employed an engine driver. Bath bricks were produced by most of the brick companies, and some 8 million were exported each year in the 1880s, 24 million in the 1890s and 17 million in the early 1900s.

Shipbuilding also continued. Fifty-one vessels were completed in the first half of the nineteenth century in seven yards, eighty-eight in the second half. Watson, Luer and Co., who produced the *Taunton Packet* in 1838, and John Gough of Crowpill who launched the *Caesarea*, a 400-ton barque in 1864, were prominent, but the only

The launch of the *Irene* in 1907

survivor by the 1890s was F.J. Carver, builder of the *Irene* in 1902. Most of the vessels, like the *Irene*, were small. In 1851 shipwrights and ships' carpenters totalled only twenty-seven; by 1881 a rather larger number included a 'vessel engineer' and a 'ship smith'.

The Bridgwater Ironworks at Dunwear, Murch's Bridgwater Foundry in Eastover, the Railway Foundry and the railway coach and wagon works employed in 1851 well over 100 people as tinplate workers, foundry men, engine fitters, moulders, brass founders and mechanics as well as general smiths. Specialist firms included James Culverwell and Co., manufacturers of brickmaking machinery, and Hennett, Spink and Else, whose most famous product was the Hampton Court Bridge, commenced in 1864.

By the late 1880s the area around the dock typified the commercial life of the town. On the north side, at the end of the Mound, were slate and marble works; to the west, beside the canal entrance, linseed and cotton cake mills and a timber yard; on the south side a saw mill, Ware's Warehouse, the Crowpill coal yard and the pottery. All yards on the south were served by the wharf and dock branch railway, cross-ing the river from the main line over the steam-driven Black or Telescopic Bridge, built in 1871.

Making lead sheeting at Henry
Bell's, Wellington Road,
c. 1957

Bridgwater docks, *c.* 1880

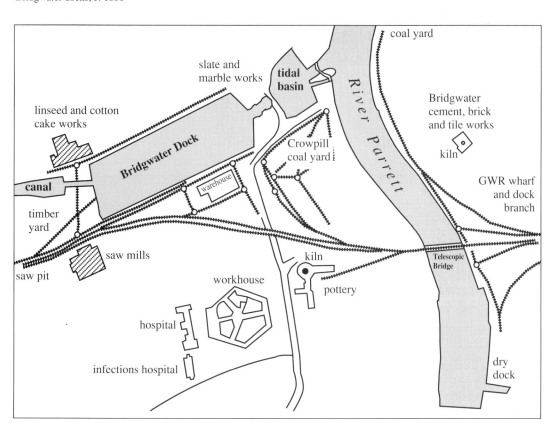

The Telescopic or Black
Bridge, opened in 1871 to carry
the dock railway

Across the bridge the branch ran along the east bank northwards to
Barham's Bridgwater Cement, Lime, Brick and Tile Works and a coal
yard; and south to a timber yard and Carver's dry dock at East Quay.
Brick works and clay pits at Hamp, Colley Lane, Dunwear, Somerset
Bridge, Castle Fields, Crowpill and Chilton spread Bridgwater's
industrial activity deep into the country.

THE PORT

In 1841 a wet dock designed by Thomas Maddicks was excavated to
the north of the town. It was linked at one end with the Bridgwater and
Taunton canal, and at the other via a tidal basin with the river. A bascule bridge and a complicated system of sluices and culverts enabled
Parrett mud to be kept at bay. Until the 1860s business in the port as a
whole did not increase much in volume from the level of the late
1820s, in spite of the inclusion of Minehead, Watchet and Porlock
within its jurisdiction in 1835. In 1855 112,395 tons were brought in
2,314 vessels, many of them coming into the port several times each

Gerald Wills watching some skilled craftsmen at Colthurst, Symons & Co.

year. By 1870, however, tonnage had almost doubled, and 1878 proved to be the record year with 233,039 tons brought in 3,864 ships.

In the 1830s and 1840s the Axfords, the Havilands, the Sullys and the firm of Stuckey and Bagehot were the most prominent in the port. All owned small, one-masted sloops and two-masted brigantines commonly used in coastal trade, as well as shallow-draught trows eminently suited to the Parrett and Tone. Charles and Frederick Axford founded the London and Bridgwater Shipping Co. in 1825 with four vessels each of about 80 tons. In 1831 they added the larger

The Tidal Basin, looking towards the former Ware's Warehouse and the modern apartments at Admiral's Quay

The barge lock and the Tidal Basin looking towards Russell Place

William the Fourth (108 tons), and in 1838 Frederick, with Robert Bagehot and others, formed the Bridgwater Steam Towing Co., which introduced the tug *Endeavour*, the first steamship in the port. The Havilands specialized in coastal business, bringing in Welsh coal and culm and also transporting limestone. The Sullys began as mariners in the eighteenth century. Thomas Sully was owner or part owner of thirty-five vessels in the 1850s, and his two sons extended the business from coastal to deep-water trade.

Stuckey and Bagehot, bankers of Langport, were shipbuilders as well as owners whose square-riggers, often bearing timber from Canada, had to discharge at Combwich. They owned the full-rigged, American-built, *British Empire*, at 1,347 tons the largest vessel registered in the port and probably intended for the timber trade between Quebec and the West Country. Unfortunately her career was short as she foundered in 1860.

By the 1860s there were about a hundred vessels registered in the port, and many more did business there. Among the smaller owners was Henry Bussell who owned the *Providence* (55 tons) which in 1863 went eighteen times to Swansea for coal, and the *Taunton Packet*

(82 tons), which in the same year came from Plymouth home to Bridgwater and then went to Cardiff, Jersey, Castletown, back to Bridgwater, and left again for Cork, Cardiff, Southampton, Newcastle, Limerick and Swansea. In contrast the *Sarah Ellen* went that year as far as Runcorn and Bordeaux; the *Mary* took iron from Cardiff to Rotterdam and copper ore from Newcastle to Swansea; and the *Little Meek* set out for the Cape of Good Hope. Tragedy overtook the *Commerce* and the *Providence*. The first was blown on shore at Burnham and was covered by eight tides, but managed to limp back to port for repairs. The second foundered with her master and two crew on Gore Sands in Bridgwater Bay.

Fewer ships were registered in the port from the 1870s, but those still finding work included the 404-ton *Paragon*, which made regular Atlantic crossings to Quebec. Henry Goodland, a young Bridgwater able seaman, served on her three times from 1874 and in ten years found himself in the Baltic, St Malo, Rouen, Bilbao, Smyrna, Patras, the Black Sea and New York. His career ended when he fell in love with a lady who refused to marry a mariner. The port suffered a serious blow when the Severn Tunnel was opened in 1885, and the railways could demonstrate that coal and other heavy goods could be moved faster and more reliably. Foreign timber and linseed for the cattle feed business, begun in 1840 by Joel Spiller, kept up imports for a time, and in 1903–4 a new quay was built for the export of bricks and tiles to Australia and New Zealand and of Bath brick to Canada, the United States, Spain, France and Germany. Most of the vessels

The Quay, *c.* 1900

involved were evidently not registered in the port, but the *Irene* called at Rotterdam in 1913, perhaps with Bath brick. A year later and such voyages would cease; but before then business fluctuated badly. In one day in 1911 only one vessel was moored in the river, although that was perhaps exceptional; total tonnage in 1912 was 108,000 tons. But the First World War interrupted what trade remained, and much of it never returned.

CHAPTER NINE

The Modern World, 1914–1992

ridgwater people knew that war had arrived when members of the town's own squadron of the West Somerset Yeomanry were billeted with their horses in many local inns. Recruiting officers must have been well pleased with the response of the town's young men to their call to the colours, but at the end of the conflict over 300 names were to be inscribed on the memorial in King Square. For those remaining behind there was some compensating prosperity: exports of bricks and tiles to the Continent obviously ceased but wages in the industry rose by 1*s* a week in 1915. Demand for wicker baskets led to a new factory in the town, and many women found employment making shirts and bandoliers for the army. Returning wounded were early anticipated, even in the euphoria of a war to be over by Christmas, and the borough council was prepared to convert the skating rink to a hospital. As the war continued beyond that date the Labour Party in particular was concerned with the sudden rise in food prices. An open-air meeting

Bridgwater Carnival Club,
1956: Nursery Fantasy

Bridgwater ladies sewing shirts in the 1950s

was memorable for a rousing speech by a young trades union organiz-
er from Bristol named Ernest Bevin.

After the war the borough council was able to turn its attention to
the problem of housing. In 1905 members of its health committee had
discovered that 534 houses were crammed together in the centre of the
town in eighty-five courts where some people lived in extreme
poverty. By 1923 those courts had been replaced by modern houses in
Newtown and Taunton Road, but slum clearance continued well into
the 1930s.

Building on this scale produced a local demand for local brick, but
in general unemployment was a serious problem. During the war,
when the Ministry of Food converted Wembdon Brewery to a fruit
pulping station, some jobs may have been created, but this and other
new firms could not find jobs for a growing labour force.
Unemployment was thought to be bad in 1924; in 1931 it was twice as
bad, in 1932 worse. In 1933 2,100 without work represented 31 per
cent of the insured population. Public works like the building of

Aneurin Bevan MP, former
Minister of Health, opens the
1,000th post-war Council
House at 10 Adscombe Avenue,
October 1953

Quantock Road in 1922 offered tempting expedients; much more satis-factory was the opening of Chilton Brickworks in 1930 which used modern manufacturing techniques for large-scale production. A triumph for the borough council was their successful encouragement of the British Cellophane Company to occupy the large site in Bath Road in 1937–8. Other small factories in Colley Lane and along Bristol Road continued the town's tradition of engineering.

More labour required more houses and improved public services. A new reservoir was opened at Ashford in 1934 and a larger one at Durleigh in 1938. At the same time there was a greater concern for public health. In 1926 the health committee of the borough council, enquiring into the forty-eight manufacturers of ice cream, were not impressed to find one operating from a pigeon house and another in a rag and bone yard. The removal of the cattle market from West Street and Penel Orlieu to a permanent site in Bath Road was further evidence of the council's concern.

It was, perhaps, natural that the council looked to extend its boundaries as the built-up area expanded into Wembdon, Durleigh and other parishes. Small pieces of land had been taken into the borough in 1835 and 1896, but in 1928 600 acres were added, and further areas in 1933, 1938 and 1952, the last addition limited after Wembdon put up a strong and successful case for retaining its independence.

National changes in the structure of local government which came into operation on All Fools' Day 1974 created a new unit of government named Sedgemoor district out of the ancient borough and the

A common Bridgwater scene: a brick and tile works in 1956

Sheep pens in West Street on market day, *c.* 1910

The *Devon*, in the docks in the 1920s

parishes which had for 80 years been Bridgwater rural district. The town's ancient corporation, founded in 1468, was thereby dissolved. Those councillors representing the area of the former borough became Charter Trustees, the guardians of Bridgwater's civic heritage.

A substantial population based on industry and commerce must have played a decisive part in the return of an Independent MP, Vernon Bartlett, at the general election in 1938 in succession to many Conservatives. A borough council representing similar views established the country's first Arts Centre in 1946 and built its 2,000th council house in 1961. But such advances were made against a background of the inevitable decline of the port. In the 1920s coal, timber, linseed, grain and hides were still imported, and the steamship *Devon* regularly sailed to Bristol, Cardiff and Newport. In the 1930s the *Parret* took over the run. But only three vessels were built in the town between 1900 and 1944, and the last sailing vessel to berth commercially at the quay came in 1934. Three years later only 1,828 cargoes came to the docks and in 1938 just 797. Economic forces were destroying the small ship; the last berthed for business above the Telescopic Bridge in 1953.

The Second World War brought two landmines to the town on 20 March 1941 which seriously damaged fifty buildings in High Street and Penel Orlieu and affected well over a thousand more. Far more damaging long-term was the closure of the docks in 1971 and the

Crane and anchor in retirement.
The dock is now a yacht marina

retreat of the railways. The conjunction of canal, river and railway which had promised so much a century earlier was outmoded. But the M5 motorway, offering the means of swift transport to London, the Midlands and the North has since 1973 enabled Bridgwater business-men to emulate their medieval predecessors. In the late 1980s land south of the town has rapidly been covered by large warehouses which play a vital part in the distribution industry of the whole country, a land port whose approaches are not governed by tides and mud flats.

Such a revolution, made possible by the internal combustion engine, could hardly have been foreseen in the 1930s when Bridgwater aspired instead to build its own airport. Cars and lorries have, of course, brought new roads in the town, often disturbing ancient sites and dam-aging ancient buildings. Bridgwater's heritage, however, still remains; hidden from all but the discerning but still, thanks to the careful custodians of its fine archives, a heritage to be read in its streets.

The problems of a modern
market town in the 1950s

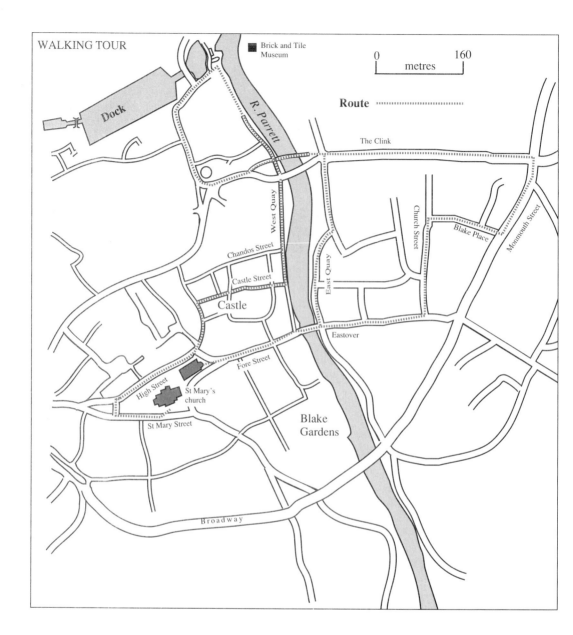

WALKING TOUR

Brick and Tile
Museum

Route

Dock

R. Parrett

The Clink

West Quay

Chandos Street

Castle Street

Castle

East Quay

Church Street

Blake Place

Monmouth Street

Eastover

Fore Street

High Street

St Mary's
church

St Mary Street

Blake
Gardens

Broadway

A Walk in the Town

The walk begins in the centre of the town at the Cornhill, the junction of High Street, Fore Street and St Mary Street.

Traders at the High Cross, *c*. 1800. The cross was erected by 1367 and was rebuilt or altered in 1567–8. By 1800 it housed a cistern for the town's water supply

The domed and pillared **Market House** was built about 1827 and is said to have been designed by John Bowen. Behind it is the **Corn Exchange** of 1875 and behind that what remains of the earlier market house of 1791. All three are still used as a covered market. Nearby in Cornhill stood the medieval **High Cross**, referred to in 1367. It was

ROBERT BLAKE
BORN IN THIS TOWN
1598
DIED AT SEA 1657

rebuilt 1567–8 and sadly demolished about 1800. It comprised an octagonal, arched structure around a central shaft providing a covered area for traders. Above the arches the building was crocketted and crenellated. The central shaft supported a cistern to which water was pumped from the Durleigh brook. Across from the High Cross, where York Buildings now stand, was the Barbican, the main entrance into the castle.

Stand on the steps of the Market House facing the statue of Robert Blake.

Notice the fine, six-bay building to your right. The date 1856 may be seen in the ornate band under the cornice.

Cross the busy street with care.

The statue of **Robert Blake,** by F.W. Pomeroy and erected in 1900, marks the beginning of the now pedestrianized Fore Street (once called 'Twixt Church and Bridge'). It is still remarkably narrow and once contained the town gaol. The shops on your left (north) are built over the castle moat. At the bottom of the street is a replica (1989) of **St Mary's Cross**, which stood in Penel Orlieu between 1769 and the 1830s.

Notice four fine dragons on a chimney of the building just by the cross, examples of the fine work produced at several of the town's brick and tile factories.

Bridgwater Bridge was opened in 1883. It was designed by R.C. Else and G.B. Laffan and was made by George Moss of Liverpool. It replaced a cast iron bridge made by Thomas Gregory of Coalbrookdale in 1795–8. That in turn replaced (on a slightly different alignment) a medieval bridge built probably by William Brewer about 1200 and rebuilt in the 1390s through a generous gift from Sir John Trivet. This was the bridge which provided the town with much of its business; the townsmen levied tolls on all goods crossing the bridge and also on goods which had to be unloaded because sea-going vessels could not pass under it.

A slipway by the bridge in Binford Place marks the site of the Langport Slip made in 1488 for traffic sailing up river. Heavy goods like iron were taken up the Parrett to Langport and along the Tone to Taunton.

The statue of Robert Blake by Pomeroy, moved from its original position and now pointing towards the river

WALKING
TOUR

The third Town Bridge, opened in 1883

Cross the bridge into Eastover.

This was the town's first suburb, which leads to the site of the medieval hospital of St John the Baptist (dissolved 1539). Nothing survives of the hospital buildings, which included a church and which housed Bridgwater's first school.

Follow Church Street and Blake Place.

These streets are part of the suburb built in the 1840s as the town expanded towards the railway. At the heart of the new development was **St John's church**, designed by John Brown of Norwich and opened in 1846. It was never finished as the architect wanted, for the spire he proposed was thought to be too heavy to be supported by Bridgwater's soft clay. The church was one of the first in the country to be planned according to the principles of the Oxford Movement.

Either return to the bridge and follow East Quay or continue into Monmouth Street and along The Clink.

East Quay provides a fine view across the river to Castle Street, the Water Gate and the surviving stretch of the castle wall, as well as of

One of the latest trains to cross the Bristol Road Bridge on its way to Edington, 28 November 1952

some of the former warehouses along the quay. The present bus station and surgery are on or near the site of the corporation's bowling green, so popular in the seventeenth century, and also near the site of the former dry dock built in the eighteenth century.

Continuing along Blake Place past St John's church into Monmouth Street, notice some elegant houses of the 1850s, not seen at their best now as the result of heavy traffic leaving the town for Bristol.

Turn left into The Clink.

Here the road follows the line of the former dock railway to the **Telescopic Bridge**, built in 1871, part of which could be drawn back to allow masted shipping to reach the quays. The bridge was last opened in 1957 and is now bereft of its machinery.

Continue to the Tidal Basin and dock.

Used for commercial purposes until 1971 this is now a marina, soon to be linked again to Taunton via the Bridgwater and Taunton canal. The basin and dock, designed by Thomas Maddicks, was opened in 1841 and is a remarkable piece of engineering. From the

Early Victorian terrace:
Church Street, Eastover,
c. 1840

Boot scraper, Church Street

river there are two entrances, one for ships and a barge lock, both giving access to the tidal basin. A second pair of gates controls the entrance to the inner basin or dock, the narrow passage crossed by a bascule bridge. A complex series of sluices and culverts was used to scour the tidal basin, which could so easily become clogged with Bridgwater's famous mud.

One of the contemporary warehouses has been converted in part to a public house and a contemporary terrace known as Russell Place overlooks the tidal basin. The terrace is decorated with two bands of local tiles.

Return to West Quay along Northgate.

One passes the base of the **Glass Cone** built by the Duke of Chandos about 1724 and demolished in 1943, before reaching West Quay. The fine house called The Lions, built by Benjamin Holloway about 1730 stands here. Its two pavilions rather lost their purpose after additions were made to the original building. West Quay was already faced and paved in 1424 and ran under the east wall of **Bridgwater Castle**. Part of that wall is exposed and the early thirteenth-century **Water Gate** is visible too, beside a restaurant of the same name.

St John's church, Eastover:
the original design, from a
lithograph of 1843

Turn right up the Duke of Chandos's elegant **Castle Street**,

The base of the Chandos Glass Kiln, erected about 1723 and demolished in 1943

designed by Holloway and built about 1724. The houses are of local brick, with ashlar dressings. The houses were a speculative development and did not sell well; the south side was probably not completed until about 1734 when the Duke of Chandos sold his interests in the town. The street houses the town's Arts Centre, one of the earliest of its kind. The street continues into **King Square** (1807–30), the site of the main buildings of the castle and the later Castle House. Thomas Baldwin, the Bath architect, submitted the first plans for the square.

> **Follow the slope from the square down into the end of High Street probably the site of the main castle entrance.**

More pleasure than business: members of Bridgwater Angling Association compete in the docks for the Bryer Cup, 1949

High Street, rebuilt in the 1820s, was the very crowded main street of the medieval town, for down its centre ran a long row of temporary shops known as the shambles since they were largely occupied by butchers. The **Town Hall**, designed in 1823 by Richard Carver, stands near the site of the **Assize Hall** (1721–1856). Many of the

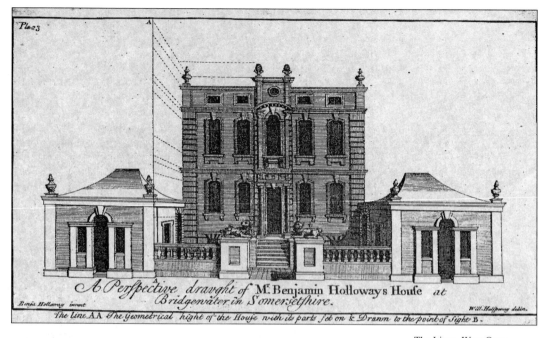

A *Perspective draught of* Mr Benjamin Holloways House *at Bridgewater in Somersetshire.*

The Lions, West Quay.
Benjamin Holloway's house
of 1730 was used in a book
to demonstrate perspective

An ornate sixteenth-century
half-timbered house in
St Mary Street,
photographed *c.* 1910

St Mary's church, *c.* 1910:
Corporation pew in south
transept

present buildings date from the 1820s and were financed by a group of
local landowners.

Proceed via Lamb Lane to The Priory.

Formerly a private house of the early eighteenth century but much
altered and extended in the nineteenth, The Priory stands in **St Mary
Street**, once very narrow because of small houses built on the edge of
the churchyard. One remaining house of the sixteenth century still
stands, thought to have been the home of the vicars of Bridgwater. A
panel shows its construction to be partly wattle-and-daub; part is of
brick. Beyond is Waterloo House, another elegant eighteenth-century
brick building, and next to it another of the sixteenth century, although
much of the timbering belongs to the 1930s.

St Mary's church, heavily restored 1849–53, remains an eloquent
expression of the prosperity of medieval Bridgwater. It is at present

open most weekday mornings and one afternoon a week. The church comprises a chancel with chapels, transepts, an aisled nave and a short western tower with an elegant spire. Drawings of the church made before restoration as well as building accounts reveal that much of the present structure was rebuilt in the later fourteenth and the fifteenth centuries to create subsidiary chapels, several of them endowed as chantries. The present pulpit and choir screens date from the early fifteenth century. From the early seventeenth century is the corporation pew, now in the south transept but originally placed in front of the chancel step.

W.H. Brakspear, the architect of the restoration, caused national controversy by his decision to change the character of the building to that of the early fourteenth century, and most of the remaining woodwork was designed by him. He planned to rebuild the tower and spire on similarly elaborate lines.

Visitors to the town are recommended to go to the **Admiral Blake Museum** in Dampiet Street where, in a building which was Blake's birthplace, the history of the town and district are displayed. There are plans to extend the premises into the adjoining Town Mill, whose history may be traced to the thirteenth century.

A second museum is under construction in East Quay which will incorporate the last of the town's brick kilns, and will tell the story of the brick and tile industry.

Barham Brothers' brick and tile kilns, *c*. 1980. One of the kilns has been restored and is to become the home of a brick and tile museum

Further Reading

Sources for most of the information given in this book and further details will be found in volume VI of the *Victoria County History of Somerset*, edited by R.W. Dunning (Oxford University Press, 1992). Two other books may be consulted:

Philip J. Squibbs, *Squibbs' History of Bridgwater*, revised and updated by John F. Lawrence (Phillimore, 1982)

Brian J. Murless, *Bridgwater Docks and the River Parrett* (Somerset County Library, 1983)

Acknowledgements

Jack Lawrence shared his deep knowledge of Bridgwater with me many years ago, when with others he attended a class which was privileged to read and discuss some of the fascinating records of the corporation. Among others who have contributed to this short study I am especially grateful to David Dawson, who commented on my archaeological speculations; to my colleague Mary Siraut, whose detailed researches into the shipping records of the port have now borne some fruit; and to Christopher Elrington, General Editor of the Victoria County Histories, with whose agreement this volume will appear at the same time as Volume VI of the *Victoria History of Somerset*, which contains a much more detailed history of the town with a full complement of references.

Picture Credits

Thanks are due to the owners of illustrations for permission to reproduce them in this book. The author is particularly grateful to David Bromwich, Local History Librarian, Taunton Castle; to 'Nick' Nicholson, Mary Thyne and Jack Gillespie at the Admiral Blake Museum, Bridgwater; To Russell Lillford of Somerset County Council; to Jeremy Dunning, whose camera here records today's Bridgwater; and to Douglas Allen, to whose retentive memory is owed some of the identifications of subjects he captured with such imagination nearly forty years ago.

Admiral Blake Museum, Bridgwater: 4, 11, 16, 25, 64, 82, 84, 91, 94 (bottom), 95, 99

Douglas Allen Photography, 17 (both), 22, 27, 32, 40, 45, 46 (bottom), 49, 68, 79, 85, 87 (top), 92, 93, 94 (top), 96 (bottom), 103, 106

Jeremy Dunning, 10, 15, 41, 61, 66, 70, 78 (both), 80, 86, 87 (bottom), 88, 96 (top), 100, 102, 105 (both), 107

National Rivers Authority, 23, 36

Geoff Roberts, 62, 110

Somerset Archaeological Society, 14, 18, 20, 29, 30, 39, 50, 67, 71, 76, 104, 108 (both), 109

Somerset County Lbrary, 44, 59, 77, 83, 89

Revd A.H. Powell, LLD, *Bridgwater in the Later Days* (1908), 19, 38, 46 (top), 58, 81

Index